GREEK
COOKING

GREEK COOKING

Rena Tambakeras

Photography by
Per Ericson

ACKNOWLEDGEMENT:

For their help, support, encouragement and patience
this book is dedicated to my husband, Graeme Patten,
our daughters Alex and Nikki and my parents
John and Carmelina Tambakeras. And in loving
memory of my Grandmother Marika Tambakeras.

Published 1987 simultaneously in Canada
and United States by Cupress,
10 Falconer Drive, Unit 8,
Mississauga, Ontario L5N 1B1

ISBN 0 920691 35 8

Printed by Mandarin Offset, Hong Kong

CONTENTS

Introduction

My interest in cooking was aroused many, many years ago. I remember my grandmother would spend many hours in the kitchen preparing the most wonderful and flavoursome meals. My mother shared her love for and enjoyment in cooking, so I was always with her learning her methods and sharing her secrets. I did not cook until my early teens when my mother for the first time in her life went to work. She would arrive home tired and would then have to prepare the evening meal. As I arrived home from school much earlier, I decided to try and prepare the meals myself. I can still see the look on my parents' face when they arrived home to my first fully prepared meal. The sheer look of surprise and pleasure would have been enough for me to try again. From then on I helped out as much as possible with the cooking.

My family has tried over the years to keep up with Greek customs and we have always enjoyed our Greek cuisine. Our kitchen was always warm and inviting with the smell of something wonderful cooking.

During the festive seasons our house is absolutely chaotic with the preparation of the festive foods and breads such as Vasilopita (New Year Bread) for New Year, Tsourekia (Easter Bread) Kourambiethes (Almond Shortbread Biscuits) Melomacaroma (Honey Dipped Cookies) for Christmas and of course the cakes and sweets for birthdays and namedays. These are given to friends and relatives and are much appreciated and enjoyed.

Greeks attach a great deal of importance to eating and food, especially when entertaining guests or celebrating the festive seasons. Greeks are renowned for their friendliness and hospitality. It is not unusual for the people to open their doors to tourists who are perfect strangers and offer them their hospitality as if they were lifelong friends. Nothing would please a Greek host more than to see a guest devour course after course. To do anything less would make your hosts feel that you are leaving the table "hungry".

In the past such meals would be prepared at leisure. With our busy lifestyles time is not always available these days. That should not mean, however, that we cannot enjoy different and exotic meals everyday. Throughout this book you will see that the recipes are simple to prepare, authentic and delicious. They are recipes that have been in my family for generations and are easy to follow and do not require you to spend hours slaving over a hot stove to achieve an authentic Greek meal. I have used time-saving methods and ingredients that are readily available.

Apart from being absolutely delicious Greek cooking is nutritious and economical to prepare.

The recipes in this book may remind you of the time you visited Greece and its beautiful islands, where you enjoyed the warm hospitality of the local people and the food served at the tavernas and restaurants whilst watching the sunset, sipping ouzo and listening to the bouzouki. For those who have not as yet had that pleasure this book will bring you a taste of Greece.

I hope you enjoy preparing and eating these recipes. I wish you KALI OREXI.

Appetizers

Mezethes

Καλή όρεχη

FRIED EGGPLANTS WITH VINEGAR

SERVES 6-8
as side dish

MELINTZANES XITHATES

	Metric/Imp.	U.S.
Medium eggplants	2	2
Salt		
Oil	500ml/1pt	2½ cups
Garlic cloves, thickly sliced	6-8	6-8
Vinegar	125ml/4fl oz	½ cup

1.

Peel three strips of skin from each eggplant lengthways.

2.

Slice eggplant in slices approximately 1.5cm/ ½" thick and sprinkle with salt, place in colander and stand for 30 minutes to drain excess moisture.

3.

Heat oil in frypan, fry eggplants until golden brown on both sides (approximately 3-4 minutes) and place in layers in deep dish.

4.

When all eggplants are cooked, discard all but 185mls/6fl oz/¾ cup oil, fry garlic until it changes colour.

5.

Remove pan from heat, pour in vinegar, gently shake frypan to mix well. Pour over eggplants. Cool, cover and refrigerate before use.

NOTE
These will keep for weeks in refrigerator and are delicious as a side dish with summer salads or on pita bread.

VARIATION
Capsicum can be prepared the same way. Using 4 whole capsicum, before frying, blanch in boiling water for 5 minutes, drain well and fry in oil, follow rest of method as above.

STUFFED CUCUMBERS

ANGOURI YEMISTO

	Metric/Imp.	U.S.
Medium-large cucumbers	4	4
Butter	125g/4oz	½ cup
Hard boiled egg, mashed	1	1
Anchovies, chopped	2	2
Slice ham, finely chopped	1	1
Freshly ground black pepper		

1.
Peel cucumbers, cut in half in middle, not lengthways.

2.
Scoop out seeds, turn upside down on paper towel to drain.

3.
Beat butter until light and fluffy, add egg, anchovies, ham and pepper, mix well.

4.
Fill cucumbers with stuffing and wrap in waxed paper and refrigerate for at least 2 hours.

5.
Cut in slices and serve as an appetizer with ouzo.

TOMATOES STUFFED WITH TUNA

SERVES 10 - 12

TOMATES YEMISTES ME TONO

	Metric/Imp.	U.S.
Tomatoes	10-12	10-12
Tuna, canned, drained	425g/15oz	15 oz
Large gherkin, chopped	1	1
Black olives, pitted and chopped	6-8	6-8
Capers	3 tsp	3 tsp
Freshly ground black pepper		
Mayonnaise (page 37)	250ml/8fl oz	1 cup
Olives and parsley for garnish		

1.
Slice tops from tomatoes and scoop out pulp, sprinkle tomato with salt, turn upside down and let excess liquid drain.

2.
Flake tuna with fork, add gherkin, olives, capers, pepper and 90g/3fl oz/⅓ cup mayonnaise.

3.
Fill each tomato (level on top) with mixture.

4.
Spread some mayonnaise on top of each tomato and garnish with half an olive and sprig of parsley.

CUCUMBER DIP

TZATZIKI

	Metric/Imp.	U.S.
Medium cucumber	1	1
Yogurt, thick plain	500g/1lb	2 cups
Vinegar	1 tsp	1 tsp
Olive oil	20ml/½fl oz	1½ tbsp
Fresh mint or dried mint	2 tsp 1½ tsp	2 tsp 1½ tsp
Cloves garlic, crushed	2	2
Salt and pepper		

1.
Peel and dice cucumber and place in strainer, stand 10 minutes to drain excess liquid.

2.
Mix cucumber with other ingredients and chill well before serving.

VARIATION
Cucumber can be peeled, seeded and grated for a finer textured dip.

FISH ROE DIP

TARAMOSALATA

	Metric/Imp.	U.S.
Fish roe (tarama)	*200g/7oz*	*7 oz*
Water	*40ml/1½fl oz*	*3 tbsp*
Medium potatoes, cooked and mashed	*3*	*3*
Olive oil	*250ml/8fl oz*	*1 cup*
Lemons, juiced	*1½*	*1½*
Small onion, grated	*1*	*1*

1.
Blend fish roe with water in electric mixer or food processor at low speed.

2.
Add slightly warm potatoes and mix well.

3.
Continue to mix gradually by adding oil alternately with lemon juice until dip becomes light and fluffy.

4.
Add grated onion—chill well before serving.

SMALL CHEESE PIES

MAKES APPROX 5 DOZ

TIROPITAKIA

	Metric/Imp.	U.S.
Feta cheese, grated	125g/4oz	4 oz
Cottage cheese	185g/6oz	¾ cup
Dried oregano or mint	1 tsp	1 tsp
Eggs, beaten	2	2
Parmesan or kefalotiri cheese, grated	25g/1oz	3 tbsp
Freshly ground black pepper		
Sheets ready rolled puff pastry	5-6	5-6
Melted butter		
Sesame seeds		
Egg, beaten, extra	1	1

1.
Mix first 6 ingredients together.

2.
Cut each pastry sheet into 9-10 rounds and place small spoonfuls of cheese mixture in centre of each circle.

3.
Fold over, press edges together, brush with beaten egg and sprinkle with sesame seeds.

4.
Place on greased trays and bake in moderately hot oven until golden brown—approximately 20 minutes. Serve hot.

NOTE

These can be prepared in advance and frozen uncooked. They keep for weeks in the freezer. Prepare as above but do not brush with beaten egg or sprinkle with sesame seeds until just before cooking.

To freeze—place Tiropitakia in single layers on baking trays and freeze, once frozen they can be placed on top of each other in either a freezer bag or plastic container.

EGGPLANT DIP

MELINTZANA PUREE

	Metric/Imp.	U.S.
Large eggplant (approximately 500g/1 lb)	1	1
Large onion, halved	1	1
Packet breadcrumbs	70g/3oz	¾ cup
Yogurt	50g/2oz	2 tbsp
Garlic cloves	2	2
Olive oil	125ml/4fl oz	½ cup
Parsley, chopped	35g/1½oz	⅓ cup
Vinegar	20ml/½fl oz	1½ tbsp
Lemon juice	20ml/½fl oz	1½ tbsp
Salt and freshly ground black pepper		

1.
Place whole eggplant on baking tray and bake in moderately hot oven for 1 hour.

2.
Remove from oven, cool slightly, peel and roughly chop.

3.
Place eggplant and all other ingredients in food processor or blender and mix until smooth.

4.
Chill overnight before serving.

5.
Serve garnished with black olives, chopped parsley and a little olive oil.

Small Cheese Pies (see p. 7)

Meat Balls (II) (see p. 98)

Fried Calamari (see p. 81)

Marinated Octopus (see p. 10)

Fried Sardines (see p. 12)

Rice-Stuffed Vine Leaves (see p. 56)

Marinated Artichokes (see p. 15)

Fish Roe Dip (centre) (see p. 6)

Cucumber Dip (centre) (see p. 5)

FRIED EGGPLANT
WITH TOMATO SAUCE

MELINTZANES TIGANITES ME TOMATA

	Metric/Imp.	U.S.
Eggplants (approx 500g/1lb each)	2	2
Vegetable oil	375ml/12fl oz	1½ cups
Olive oil	80ml/3fl oz	⅓ cup
Large onion, grated	1	1
Garlic cloves, grated	3	3
Peeled, canned tomatoes, finely chopped	500g/1lb	2 cups
Parsley, chopped	50g/2oz	½ cup
Salt and pepper		
Water	80ml/3fl oz	⅓ cup
Plain yogurt		

1.

Peel three strips off eggplant lengthways. Cut into slices 1cm/½" thick, sprinkle with salt and stand 1 hour.

2.

Fry eggplant slices a few at a time in hot vegetable oil until brown both sides. Drain on paper towel. Add more oil if needed. Discard used oil.

3.

Heat olive oil and fry onion and garlic until onion is soft and begins to change colour.

4.

Add tomatoes with liquid, parsley, salt, pepper and water. Cook approximately 10 minutes until sauce thickens.

5.

Arrange layers of eggplants and sauce in bowl and refrigerate overnight before serving with yogurt as a side dish or in pita bread.

NOTE
This dish will keep in refrigerator up to 1 week and flavour improves as age increases.

Fried Eggplant with Tomato Sauce

MARINATED OCTOPUS

OKTAPOTHI XITHATO

	Metric/Imp.	U.S.
Small octopus	*1kg/2lb*	*2 lb*
Olive oil	*125ml/4fl oz*	*½ cup*
Vinegar	*60ml/2fl oz*	*¼ cup*
Oregano	*3 tsp*	*3 tsp*
Salt and freshly ground black pepper		

1.
Wash octopus, remove any thick skin, inkbag, eyes etc.

2.
Rinse well and boil in water until tender, drain.

3.
Chop into bite-sized pieces, place in bowl.

4.
Add other ingredients, mix well and refrigerate overnight before serving.

NOTE

Octopus prepared this way keeps for several days in the refrigerator and taste improves with age. Vary the amount of other ingredients to suit your taste.

SAVOURY STICKS

MAKES APPROX 70

BATON SALE

	Metric/Imp.	U.S.
Butter, melted	125g/4oz	½ cup
Oil	125ml/4fl oz	½ cup
Lukewarm water	125ml/4fl oz	½ cup
Freshly cracked pepper	3-4 tsp	3-4 tsp
Salt	½-1 tsp	½-1 tsp
Self-raising flour	300g/10oz	2¼ cups
Cumin powder	2 tsp	2 tsp
Sesame seeds	3 tsp	3 tsp
Cumin seeds	25g/1oz	3 tbsp
Sesame seeds, extra		

1.
Combine first 8 ingredients into soft dough—knead 2-3 minutes.

2.
Roll pieces of dough into pencil-sized sticks approximately 15cm/6" long—twist.

3.
Place on well greased and floured baking trays, sprinkle liberally with extra sesame seeds and cumin seeds.

4.
Bake in moderate-hot oven 15 minutes until golden brown.

5.
Cool completely before storing in airtight container.

FRIED SARDINES

SERVES 4 - 6

SARTHELES TIGANITES

	Metric/Imp.	U.S.
Fresh sardines or whitebait	1kg/2lb	2 lb
Salt		
Flour		
Oil		

1.

Wash sardines, sprinkle with salt.

2.

Roll in flour and fry in hot oil until golden brown, 2-3 minutes.

3.

Serve hot sprinkled with lemon juice. Great as part of "Meze".

SPICY LOAF

PITA ALMIRI

	Metric/Imp.	U.S.
Eggs	6	6
Butter	*200g/7oz*	*¾ cup*
Parmesan or kefalotiri cheese, grated	*100g/3oz*	*¾ cup*
Mortadella, diced	*250g/8oz*	*8 oz*
Black olives, pitted	*10-12*	*10-12*
Salt and freshly ground black pepper		
Self-raising flour	*200g/7oz*	*1 ⅔ cups*

1.
Beat eggs and butter until creamy.

2.
Add cheese, mortadella, olives, salt and pepper and mix.

3.
Gradually add flour, blend together and place in buttered and floured loaf tin.

4.
Bake in moderately hot oven for approximately 1 hour until golden brown.

5.
Cool, slice.

6.
Serve warm or cold.

ANCHOVIES

ANCHOUYES

	Metric/Imp.	U.S.
Anchovies, dried and salted	*250g/8oz*	*8 oz*
Olive oil	*125ml/4fl oz*	*½ cup*
Dark vinegar	*60ml/2fl oz*	*¼ cup*

1.

Trim and fillet anchovies, wash very well under cold water and rinse off all traces of salt.

2.

Place in small elongated dish. Pour oil and vinegar on top and gently mix.

3.

Allow to stand 1 hour before serving on salad or part of "Meze".

NOTE

Cover and refrigerate when not used. Will keep in refrigerator for 3-4 weeks. Should oil solidify in fridge, leave to stand at room temperature for at least 1 hour before serving.

MARINATED ARTICHOKES

ANGINARES XITHATES

	Metric/Imp.	U.S.
Artichoke hearts, canned	400g/14oz	14 oz
Garlic cloves, halved	2	2
Olive oil	125ml/4fl oz	½ cup
Vinegar	60ml/2fl oz	¼ cup
Oregano	1½ tsp	1½ tsp
Freshly ground black pepper		
Salt		

1.

Drain artichoke hearts, place in glass jar and add other ingredients.

2.

Cover and gently shake to mix all ingredients.

3.

Place in refrigerator and stand 24 hours before use.

NOTE

Artichokes will keep in refrigerator in jar for several weeks and are delicious in salads and served as part of "Meze".

MUSHROOMS IN OUZO

MANITARIA ME OUZO

	Metric/Imp.	U..S.
Mushrooms	250g/8oz	8 oz
Black olives	8-10	8-10
Olive oil	60ml/2fl oz	¼ cup
Garlic cloves, crushed	1	1
Lemon, juiced	½	½
Oregano	½ tsp	½ tsp
Hot chilli pepper	¼ tsp	¼ tsp
Ouzo	30ml/1fl oz	2 tbsp
Parsley, chopped	35g/1½oz	⅓ cup
Salt and freshly ground black pepper		

1.
Wash, dry and finely slice mushrooms. Place in bowl with olives.

2.
Combine other ingredients and pour over mushrooms, gently mix.

3.
Chill overnight before serving.

SPICY CAPSICUMS

PIPERIES ME KIMINO

	Metric/Imp.	U.S.
Capsicum, washed, cored and cut into 4	6	6
Olive oil	80ml/3fl oz	⅓ cup
Garlic cloves, crushed	4-5	4-5
Cumin powder	1 tsp	1 tsp
Vinegar	60ml/2fl oz	¼ cup
Salt and freshly ground black pepper		

1.

Grill/broil capsicum for approximately 15 minutes each side until skin darkens and bubbles. Peel skin, place in serving dish.

2.

Heat oil, gently fry garlic until it starts to darken.

3.

Add cumin, stir, add vinegar, mix and pour over capsicum.

4.

Add salt and pepper, mix gently, cover and refrigerate overnight before serving.

Salads

Salates

Καλή όρεχη

VILLAGE TOMATO SALAD

SALATA HORIATIKI

	Metric/Imp.	U.S.
Large tomatoes	4	4
Shallots, sliced	4	4
Feta cheese, cubed	150g/5oz	5oz
Black olives	8-10	8-10
Olive oil	80ml/3fl oz	⅓ cup
Vinegar	30ml/1fl oz	2 tbsp
Oregano	1 tsp	1 tsp
Salt and pepper		

1.
Cut tomatoes into wedges and place in bowl with other ingredients, toss.

2.
Serve with crusty bread.

VARIATION
Substitute 1 large sliced onion for shallots.

TUNA SALAD

S E R V E S   6 - 8

SALATA APO TONO

	Metric/Imp.	U.S.
Lettuce leaves		
Tuna, canned	425ml/15oz	15 oz
Medium potatoes, boiled	4	4
Medium tomatoes	2	2
Capsicum, sliced into rings	1	1
Marinated artichokes (see recipe page 15)		
Cucumber, sliced	1	1
Onion, sliced	1	1
Shallots, sliced	2	2
Black olives		

DRESSING

Olive oil	80ml/3fl oz	⅓ cup
Vinegar	40ml/1½fl oz	3 tbsp
Capers	3 tsp	3 tsp
Salt and pepper		

1.
Garnish serving bowl with lettuce leaves.

2.
Quarter potatoes and tomatoes lengthways and arrange on serving bowl with other ingredients.

3.
Mix dressing ingredients together and pour over salad.

MAYONNAISE SALAD

SERVES 6 - 8
as side dish

SALATA ROSSIKI

	Metric/Imp.	U.S.
Beetroot slices	6	6
Dried white beans, cooked	200g/7oz	1 cup
Potatoes, boiled and cubed	3	3
Carrots, boiled and cubed	3	3
Peas, cooked	125g/4 oz	1 cup
Gherkins, chopped	2	2
Black olives, chopped	8	8
Salt and pepper		
Olive oil	40ml/1½fl oz	3 tbsp
Mayonnaise (page 37)	375ml/12fl oz	1½ cups

1.

Dry beetroot on absorbent paper and cut into small pieces.

2.

Mix all ingredients with 125m/4fl oz/½ cup mayonnaise.

3.

Place in deep serving dish and spread remainder of mayonnaise over vegetables and garnish.

NOTE

Slices of hard boiled egg, carrots, olives, gherkins, capers, peas etc can be used for garnishing. For a quick Salata Rossiki substitute beans, potatoes, carrots and peas with 1kg/2lb frozen vegetables cooked, then follow method as above.

RICE SALAD
SERVES 6 - 8

SALATA APO RIZI

	Metric/Imp.	U.S.
Boiled Rice	600g/1¼lb	3 cups
Gherkins, chopped	2	2
Salami, diced	125g/4oz	½ cup
Capsicum, chopped	½	½
Carrots, grated	2	2
Corn kernels, cooked	125g/4oz	¾ cup
Small onion, grated	1	1
Shallots, finely chopped	4	4
Parsley, chopped	35g/1½oz	⅓ cup
Peas, cooked	125g/4oz	¾ cup
Large lemon, juiced	1	1
Vinegar	3 tsp	3 tsp
Olives, pitted and chopped	8-10	8-10
Olive oil	80ml/3fl oz	⅓ cup
Salt and pepper		

1.
Mix all ingredients together.

2.
Place in ring-form pan, chill at least 2 hours.

3.
Turn out onto a serving dish and garnish centre with chopped tomatoes and black olives.

GREEK SALAD

SALATA

	Metric/Imp.	U.S.
Lettuce, preferably cos	1	1
Firm tomatoes	2	2
Cucumber, sliced	1	1
Green capsicum, sliced	1	1
Shallots, chopped	6	6
Radishes, sliced	3-4	3-4
Feta cheese, cubed	125g/4oz	4 oz
Black olives	12-15	12-15
Anchovy fillets	6-8	6-8
Onion, sliced	1	1

DRESSING

	Metric/Imp.	U.S.
Olive oil	125ml/4fl oz	½ cup
Vinegar	60ml/2fl oz	¼ cup
Oregano	2 tsp	2 tsp
Garlic cloves, crushed	2	2
Salt and pepper		

1.
Wash lettuce and shake off excess liquid, tear into small pieces. Cut tomatoes into 6 wedges each.

2.
Arrange lettuce and other ingredients in salad bowl.

3.
Mix dressing ingredients together and pour over salad, toss gently and serve.

Greek Salad

PRAWN SALAD
SERVES 4

SALATA APO GARITHES

	Metric/Imp.	U.S.
Cooked prawns	500g/1lb	1 lb
Parsley, chopped	35g/1½oz	⅓ cup
Olive oil	80ml/3fl oz	⅓ cup
Lemon juice	60ml/2fl oz	¼ cup
Salt and freshly ground black pepper		
Black olives (optional)	10	10

1.
Devein prawns, place in bowl.

2.
Add other ingredients, mix well.

3.
Chill for at least 2 hours before serving.

Prawn Salad

ZUCCHINI SALAD

KOLOKITHAKIA SALATA

	Metric/Imp.	U.S.
Small zucchini, thickly sliced	1kg/2lb	2 lb
Garlic cloves, crushed	2	2
Parsley, chopped	50g/2oz	½ cup
Olive oil	125ml/4fl oz	½ cup
Lemon, juiced	½-1	½-1
Salt and pepper		

1.
Boil zucchini in salted water until just tender, drain.

2.
Place in serving bowl, mix other ingredients, pour over zucchini, toss gently. Chill before serving.

CHICORY SALAD

HORTA

	Metric/Imp.	U.S.
Bunch chicory	1	1
Olive oil	60ml/2fl oz	¼ cup
Lemon juice to taste		
Salt		

1.
Trim leaves and stems, wash very carefully under cold running water.

2.
Place in large saucepan with boiling salted water and cook until tender.

3.
Drain, place in bowl and add other ingredients.

4.
Serve hot or cold with fish dishes.

NOTE
After chicory is drained, the water can be reserved, cooled and drunk with a squeeze of lemon juice. It is delicious and supposedly very good for cleansing the kidneys.

BEETROOT SALAD

PANTZARIA SALATA

	Metric/Imp.	U.S.
Sliced beetroot, drained	425g/15oz	15 oz
Garlic cloves, crushed	2	2
Olive oil	80ml/3fl oz	⅓ cup
Vinegar	40ml/1½fl oz	3 tbsp
Salt and pepper		

1.
Place beetroot in bowl.

2.
Combine all other ingredients and pour over beetroot. Chill and serve.

GREEN BEAN SALAD

FASSOLAKIA SALATA

	Metric/Imp.	U.S.
Green beans	500g/1lb	1 lb
Garlic cloves, crushed	2	2
Olive oil	80ml/3fl oz	⅓ cup
Lemon, juiced	½-1	½-1
Salt and pepper		

1.
Trim and string beans, cut into 2 or 3 pieces.

2.
Boil in salted water until tender, drain and cool.

3.
Mix all ingredients and pour over beans. Chill before serving.

NOTE
Beans prepared this way can also be served warm and/or with Skorthalia Sauce (Page 36).

POTATO SALAD

SERVES 4-6

PATATOSALATA

	Metric/Imp.	U.S.
Large tomatoes	3	3
Potatoes, boiled and peeled	1kg/2lb	2 lb
Large onions, sliced	2	2
Black olives	12	12
Vinegar	60ml/2fl oz	¼ cup
Olive oil	125ml/4fl oz	½ cup
Salt and pepper		
Parsley, chopped		

1.
Cut tomatoes into six wedges each and cold potatoes into quarters.

2.
Arrange potatoes, tomatoes, onions and olives in bowl.

3.
Mix vinegar, oil, salt and pepper together and pour over salad, sprinkle with chopped parsley and serve.

CHICK PEA SALAD

REVITHIA SALATA

	Metric/Imp.	U.S.
Dried chick peas	375ml/13oz	2 cups
Onion, chopped	1	1
Shallots, finely chopped	4	4
Parsley, chopped	35g/1½oz	⅓ cup
Olive oil	80ml/3fl oz	⅓ cup
Vinegar	60ml/2fl oz	¼ cup
Salt and freshly ground black pepper		

1.
Wash peas, cover with water and soak overnight. Drain.

2.
Place peas in saucepan, cover with fresh water and bring to boil, reduce heat and simmer until tender — approximately 1 hour. Drain.

3.
Place in bowl and cool.

4.
Add remaining ingredients, toss. Chill before serving.

CAULIFLOWER SALAD

KOUNOUPITHI SALATA

	Metric/Imp.	U.S.
Small cauliflower	1	1
Parsley, chopped	50g/2oz	½ cup
Garlic cloves, crushed	2-3	2-3
Olive oil	125ml/4fl oz	½ cup
Lemon, juiced	1	1
Salt and pepper		

1.
Cut stem off cauliflower and cut into small flowerettes.

2.
Place in salted boiling water and cook until tender. Drain and cool.

3.
Add cauliflower to other ingredients, toss. Chill before serving.

EGGPLANT SALAD

MELINTZANOSALATA

	Metric/Imp.	U.S.
Large eggplants	2	2
Garlic cloves, crushed	2	2
Parsley, chopped	35g/1½oz	⅓ cup
Olive oil	80ml/3fl oz	⅓ cup
Vinegar	30ml/1fl oz	2 tbsp
Salt and pepper		

1.

Remove stem, wash and peel three strips off each eggplant. Cut in half lengthways, remove seeds and cube.

2.

Place in salted boiling water and cook until tender, drain and cool.

3.

Place in bowl with other ingredients, toss and serve.

Sauces

Saltses

Καλή όρεχη

GARLIC SAUCE

SKORTHALIA

	Metric/Imp.	U.S.
Hot water	30ml/1fl oz	2 tbsp
Medium potatoes, boiled and mashed	2	2
Garlic cloves, crushed	5	5
Salt	1 tsp	1 tsp
Olive oil	125ml/4fl oz	½ cup
Lemon juice	60ml/2fl oz	¼ cup

1.
Add water to mashed potatoes, mix in garlic and salt.

2.
Gradually blend in oil and lemon, beat well until smooth and light.

3.
Cover and chill.

MAYONNAISE
MAKES 2 CUPS

MAYONNEZA

	Metric/Imp.	U.S.
Egg yolks	2	2
Vinegar	1 tsp	1 tsp
Dry mustard	1½ tsp	1½ tsp
Salt and pepper		
Small potatoes, boiled and mashed	2	2
Lemon juice	60ml/2fl oz	¼ cup
Olive oil	250ml/8fl oz	1 cup

1.
Beat egg yolks with vinegar and add mustard, salt and pepper.

2.
Beat well and add potato, beat again.

3.
Slowly add lemon juice alternating with oil and beat until mayonnaise thickens. If mayonnaise separates, slowly add 3 tsp hot water and mix well.

NOTE
Potatoes should be boiled in their jackets then peeled and mashed. For a light fluffy mayonnaise, prepare while potatoes are still warm.

EGG AND LEMON SAUCE

AVGOLEMONO

	Metric/Imp.	U.S.
Butter	50g/2oz	3 tbsp
Flour	25g/1oz	3 tbsp
Stock	450ml/14fl oz	1¾ cups
Milk	60ml/2fl oz	¼ cup
Egg yolks	2	2
Lemons, juiced	1-1½	1-1½
Salt and pepper		

1.
Melt butter in saucepan and remove from heat. Stir in flour to make smooth paste and return to heat.

2.
Slowly add milk and cooled stock, stirring constantly until sauce thickens.

3.
Beat egg yolks with lemon juice and slowly pour into mixture, stir constantly until boiling, cook further 1 minute.

4.
Add salt and pepper and serve immediately.

OIL AND LEMON DRESSING

LATHOLEMONO

	Metric/Imp.	U.S.
Olive oil	185ml/6fl oz	¾ cup
Lemon juice	60ml/2fl oz	¼ cup
Oregano	1 tsp	1 tsp
Salt and freshly ground black pepper		
Parsley, finely chopped	2 tsp	2 tsp

1.
Blend all ingredients together until well mixed.

2.
Stand for 1 hour before use.

NOTE
This dressing is delicious poured over seafood such as fresh prawns, lobster or grilled fish. This dressing keeps for up to two weeks in a jar with lid in the refrigerator.

39

WHITE CREAM SAUCE

CREMA BECHAMEL

	Metric/Imp.	U.S.
Butter	*75g/3oz*	*⅓ cup*
Flour	*50g/2oz*	*6 tbsp*
Milk	*1ltr/2pts*	*4½ cups*
Eggs	*3*	*3*
Parmesan or kefalotiri cheese, grated	*60g/2oz*	*½ cup*
Salt and pepper		

1.
Melt butter in saucepan, remove from heat and add flour, stirring to a smooth paste.

2.
Return to medium heat and slowly add milk, stirring constantly until sauce begins to bubble and thicken.

3.
Cook 1-2 minutes, remove from heat and allow to cool slightly.

4.
Add eggs one at a time to sauce and stir quickly.

5.
Return to heat and add cheese, salt and pepper and mix well.

6.
Cook further 1-2 minutes until mixture bubbles.

Soups

Soupes

Καλή όρεχη

GREEN LENTIL SOUP

SERVES 4 - 6

MAVRI FAKI SOUPA

	Metric/Imp.	U.S.
Lentils	375g/13oz	2 cups
Large onion, chopped	1	1
Peeled tomato, chopped	1	1
Capsicum, chopped	½	½
Tomato paste	30g/1oz	1½ tbsp
Celery stalk, sliced	1	1
Carrots, sliced	2	2
Garlic cloves, chopped	2	2
Bay leaves	2	2
Olive oil	60ml/2fl oz	¼ cup
Salt and pepper		
Water	1¾ltrs/3½pts	7½ cups

EXTRA

Olive oil	40ml/1fl oz	3 tbsp
Onion, grated	1	1
Garlic cloves, crushed	3	3
Cumin powder	2 tsp	2 tsp
Vinegar		

1.

Clean and wash lentils, remove any stones.

2.

Place in pan, cover with water, boil 5 minutes and drain.

3.

Add other ingredients to lentils in saucepan, cover and bring to boil, simmer 1-1¼ hours until lentils are soft.

4.

Heat olive oil and fry onion and garlic. Add cumin powder and stir well.

5.

Pour into hot lentil soup and serve sprinkled with vinegar to taste, crusty bread and freshly sliced onion.

RED LENTIL SOUP

SERVES 4 - 6

KOKINI FAKI SOUPA

	Metric/Imp.	U.S.
Red lentils	375g/13oz	2 cups
Bay leaf	1	1
Ripe tomatoes, peeled and chopped	2	2
Onion, chopped	1	1
Garlic cloves, chopped	2	2
Salt and pepper		
Water	1½ ltrs/3pts	7 cups
Oil	40ml/1½fl oz	3 tbsp

GARNISH

	Metric/Imp.	U.S.
Olive oil	60ml/2fl oz	¼ cup
Onion, grated	1	1
Cloves garlic, crushed	3	3
Cumin	1 tsp	1 tsp

1.
Clean and wash lentils, place in saucepan with other ingredients and bring to boil, reduce heat and cook for 45 minutes until lentils are cooked and soup thickens.

2.
Remove from heat and discard bay leaf. Cool.

3.
Blend in food processor.

4.
Garnish—heat oil, saute onion and garlic, add cumin and mix well. Pour into lentil soup.

5.
Serve with crusty bread.

CAULIFLOWER SOUP

SERVES 4-6

SOUPA APO KOUNOUPITHI

	Metric/Imp.	U.S.
Small cauliflower	½	½
Olive oil	60ml/2fl oz	¼ cup
Onions, chopped	2	2
Peeled, canned tomatoes, chopped	500g/1lb	2 cups
Medium potatoes, chopped	2	2
Parsley, chopped	25g/1oz	¼ cup
Small macaroni	200g/7oz	7 oz
Salt and pepper		
Eggs, beaten	2	2
Parmesan cheese, grated	60g/2oz	½ cup

1.
Chop cauliflower into small pieces.

2.
Heat oil and brown onion, add tomatoes, potatoes, parsley, cauliflower and cover with water.

3.
Cook, covered until potatoes and cauliflower are almost tender.

4.
Add macaroni, salt, pepper, eggs and grated cheese.

5.
Cook further 15-20 minutes until macaroni are tender.

6.
Serve hot with crusty bread.

WHITE BEAN SOUP

FASSOLATHA

SERVES 4-6

	Metric/Imp.	U.S.
Dried white cannellini beans	375g/13oz	2 cups
Water, for soaking	2ltrs/4pts	9 cups
Olive oil	80ml/3fl oz	1/3 cup
Large onion, halved and sliced	1	1
Garlic cloves, chopped	3	3
Smoked bacon bones	250g/8oz	8 oz
Medium carrots, sliced	4	4
Celery stalks with leaves, sliced	2	2
Peeled, canned tomatoes, chopped	500g/1lb	2 cups
Tomato paste	30g/1oz	1½ tbsp
Freshly ground black pepper		
Water	1½ltrs/3pts	7 cups
Zucchini, sliced	3	3
Parsley, chopped	50g/2oz	½ cup

1.
Soak beans overnight in water, drain.

2.
Heat oil, saute onion and garlic.

3.
Add bacon bones, carrots, celery, tomatoes, tomato paste and cook 2 minutes.

4.
Add beans, pepper and water, cook on low heat covered 1½ hours.

5.
Add zucchini and parsley, turn heat to medium, cook further 30 minutes until beans are tender.

6.
Serve with fresh crusty bread and raw peeled and quartered onions. This soup can also be eaten cold.

VARIATION
This dish can be prepared as a vegetarian dish by omitting bacon. If using black eyed beans do not soak. Cooking time may vary as these are more tender.

CARMELINA'S EASTER SOUP

SERVES 6-8

MAYIRITSA

	Metric/Imp.	U.S.
Lamb, cut into strips	500g/1lb	1 lb
Tripe, cut into strips	1kg/2lb	2 lb
Calves liver, cut into strips	400g/14oz	14 oz
Large onions, halved and sliced	3	3
Butter, melted	125g/4oz	½ cup
Water	1½ ltrs/3pts	7 cups
Salt and pepper		
Lemons, juiced	4	4
Egg yolks	6	6

1.
Wash lamb, tripe and liver and place in colander, drain.

2.
Place in saucepan on high heat and cook until all moisture evaporates.

3.
Add onions, stir, add butter and cook until onions are soft.

4.
Add water, salt and pepper and cover. Cook on medium heat approximately 1 hour until meat is tender. Cool.

5.
Beat lemon juice and egg yolks and pour into soup, stir. Cook 2-3 minutes and serve.

NOTE

This soup is traditionally eaten just after midnight on Easter Saturday after everyone returns from church to a feast (early Easter Sunday) to signify the end of Lent. Traditionally the soup is made up from intestines, head, lungs and heart of young lamb. I can remember my grandmother preparing it this way but since my mother took over the task of preparing this once a year soup, she has departed from using these ingredients and instead has used ingredients that most people would find more acceptable. The result is simply delicious and the taste almost identical to the traditional dish.

FISH SOUP
WITH EGG & LEMON

S E R V E S   4 - 6

PSAROSOUPA

	Metric/Imp.	U.S.
Fish	1kg/2lb	2 lb
Large carrots, sliced	4	4
Zucchini, chopped	4	4
Potatoes, sliced	3	3
Celery stalks with leaves, chopped	4	4
Ripe tomatoes, halved	2	2
Large onion, quartered	1	1
Salt and pepper		
Water	2¼ ltrs/4½ pts	10 cups
Rice	60g/2oz	¼ cup
Egg yolks	2	2
Lemons, juiced	1-1½	1-1½

1.
Clean fish, cut into pieces leaving head on and set aside.

2.
Place other ingredients except rice, egg yolks and lemon juice, in large saucepan, bring to boil and simmer 50 minutes.

3.
Add fish, simmer 15 minutes until fish is cooked.

4.
Remove fish, set aside.

5.
Strain soup, puree vegetables and return to soup. Bring to boil, reduce heat.

6.
Add rice, simmer 15-20 minutes until rice cooked.

7.
Beat egg yolks with lemon juice and add to slightly cooled soup, stirring briskly.

8.
Heat soup 2-3 minutes, stirring regularly. Serve.

NOTE

Fish can be deboned, cut into small pieces and served in the soup *or* fish can be served separately sprinkled with lemon juice, olive oil and cracked pepper.

47

THICK CHICKEN SOUP
WITH EGG & LEMON

SERVES 4

KOTOSOUPA AVGOLEMONO

	Metric/Imp.	U.S.
Chicken	1.5kg/3lb	3 lb
Large onion, quartered	1	1
Carrots, halved	2	2
Tomato, quartered	1	1
Celery stalks with leaves, halved	2	2
Zucchini, halved	2	2
Potato, quartered	1	1
Water	1¼ ltrs/2½pts	6 cups
Salt and pepper		
Rice	60g/2oz	¼ cup
Egg yolks	2	2
Lemons, juiced	1-1½	1-1½

1.
Place all ingredients except rice, egg yolks and lemon juice in large saucepan and bring to boil.

2.
Reduce heat and simmer, covered 1-1¼ hours, until chicken is cooked.

3.
Remove chicken, blend drained vegetables in blender or food processor and return pureed vegetables to stock.

4.
Bring to boil, add rice and cook until rice is tender — 15-20 minutes. Remove from heat and cool.

5.
Beat egg yolks and lemon juice, gradually add 250ml/8fl oz/1 cup of stock and mix well.

6.
Pour egg mixture into soup, stirring constantly. Return to medium heat and cook for 1 or 2 minutes, heat through and serve.

VARIATION

1.
Chicken can be cut up and served in soup.

2.
Place chicken in oven with a little butter and roast.

3.
Use chicken in Chicken Pie (Page 138).

SPLIT PEA SOUP

SERVES 4

FAVA

	Metric/Imp.	U.S.
Yellow split peas	500g/1lb	2⅔ cups
Large onion, quartered	1	1
Garlic cloves, halved	3	3
Olive oil	80ml/3fl oz	⅓ cup
Salt and pepper		

1.

Wash split peas, discard any stones or discoloured peas, place in saucepan, cover with water and bring to boil.

2.

Boil for 5-10 minutes, remove scum from liquid and add onion and garlic, simmer for 1-1½ hours until peas are tender.

3.

Put through blender or food processor, adding olive oil.

4.

Return to heat, add salt and pepper. Serve.

NOTE

This is a very thick soup.

THICK BEEF SOUP

SERVES 4-6

KREATOSOUPA

	Metric/Imp.	U.S.
Stewing beef	1kg/2lb	2 lb
Soup bones with marrow	2	2
Large onion, quartered	1	1
Carrots, halved	2	2
Tomatoes, quartered	2	2
Celery stalks with leaves, halved	2	2
Zucchini, halved	3	3
Potatoes, quartered	2	2
Water	1¾ltrs/3½pts	7½ cups
Salt and pepper		
Rice	60g/2oz	¼ cup
Lemon, juiced	½	½

1.
Cut beef into 3-4 pieces, place in large saucepan with all other ingredients except rice and lemon juice.

2.
Bring to boil, remove any scum from soup, reduce heat and cook 1-1½ hours until meat is tender.

3.
Remove meat and bones from soup.

4.
Strain vegetables, put through food processor or blender, return to stock.

5.
Heat, add rice and cook until rice is tender— 15-20 minutes.

6.
Cut meat into small serving pieces, add to soup, heat and serve sprinkled with lemon juice.

EGG AND LEMON SOUP

SERVES 4

SOUPA AVGOLEMONO

	Metric/Imp.	U.S.
Chicken or fish stock	1¾ltrs/3½pts	7½ cups
Rice	50g/2oz	⅓ cup
Egg yolks	2	2
Lemons, juiced	1-1½	1-1½
Salt and pepper		

1.

Bring stock to boil, add rice and boil gently until rice is tender, 15-20 minutes. Cool slightly.

2.

Beat egg yolks and lemon juice, add salt and pepper.

3.

Gradually add 250ml/8fl oz/1 cup stock to eggs, stirring constantly and briskly.

4.

Pour egg mixture into remaining stock. Stir well, heat through over low heat. Serve.

MEAT BALL SOUP
S E R V E S 4

YOUVERLAKIA

	Metric/Imp.	U.S.
Minced ground beef	500g/1lb	1 lb
Rice	50g/2oz	⅓ cup
Onion, grated	1	1
Garlic cloves, crushed	2	2
Parsley, chopped	3 tsp	3 tsp
Egg	1	1
Salt and pepper		
Water	1¼ltrs/2pts	5 cups
Onion, chopped, extra	1	1
Tomato, chopped	1	1
Butter	25g/1oz	1½ tbsp
Egg yolks	2	2
Lemon, juiced	1	1
Semolina	3 tsp	3 tsp

1.
Mix first seven ingredients together and shape into small balls.

2.
Bring water to boil with extra onion, tomato and butter. Cook 15 minutes. Add meat balls and simmer until meat is tender, 30-40 minutes—remove from heat and cool.

3.
Beat egg yolks with lemon juice.

4.
Pour 1 cup of stock into eggs slowly, beating well, add semolina—mix.

5.
Pour eggs into soup and return to low heat for few minutes, gently stirring until soup thickens. Serve hot.

NOTE
This is a thick soup.

Vegetarian

Hortofagia

Καλή όρεχη

STUFFED ARTICHOKES

SERVES 6

ANGINARES YEMISTES

	Metric/Imp.	U.S.
Artichokes	6	6
Oil	60ml/2fl oz	¼ cup

STUFFING

	Metric/Imp.	U.S.
Rice	250g/8oz	1¼ cups
Tomatoes, grated	2	2
Onion, grated	1	1
Fennel, chopped	35g/1½oz	⅓ cup
Olive oil	125ml/4fl oz	½ cup
Salt and pepper		

1.
Wash artichokes, cut off stems close to base, trim tops and sharp leaf ends with scissors.

2.
Bash artichokes on chopping board, face down, to spread leaves. Spread centre leaves as much as possible and scrape off choke.

3.
Mix all stuffing ingredients and fill centres of artichokes with stuffing.

4.
Place close together, standing up, in saucepan with oil and water (water should come to about 1.5cm/½" below top of artichokes).

5.
Bring to boil, reduce heat and cook approximately 45 minutes or until rice is cooked.

SMALL STUFFED EGGPLANTS

SERVES 6 - 10
as appetizer

MELINTZANES YEMISTES NISTISIMES

	Metric/Imp.	U.S.
Small eggplants (approx. 5cm/2" long)	1kg/2lb	2 lb
Olive oil	185ml/6fl oz	¾ cup
Large onions, halved and sliced	3	3
Garlic cloves, crushed	4	4
Peeled, canned tomatoes, chopped	500g/1lb	2 cups
Parsley, chopped	50g/2oz	½ cup
Salt and pepper		
Water	80ml/3fl oz	⅓ cup

1.

Make 3 incisions lengthways in each eggplant, rub inside each with salt and stand at least 1 hour to remove bitterness and drain excess moisture.

2.

Heat oil and gently fry eggplants on all sides until just soft then remove from frypan.

3.

Add onion and garlic to pan, fry until soft then add tomatoes, parsley, salt, pepper and water.

4.

Cook for 10-15 minutes until mixture thickens. Remove from heat.

5.

Stuff some of mixture into incisions in eggplants and place in baking dish close together, in one layer and pour any remaining stuffing on top.

6.

Cover with foil and cook in moderate oven 40-50 minutes.

7.

Serve hot or cold as a side dish.

VARIATION
Chilli powder can be added to stuffing mixture.

55

RICE-STUFFED VINE LEAVES

SERVES 4-6

DOLMATHES LATHERES

	Metric/Imp.	U.S.
Grape vine leaves	200g/7oz	7 oz
Rice	300g/10oz	1¼ cups
Medium onions, grated	2	2
Large tomatoes, grated, reserve skins	2	2
Fresh mint, chopped	3-4 tsp	3-4 tsp
Salt and pepper		
Olive oil	125ml/4fl oz	½ cup
Water	500ml/1pt	2½ cups
Olive oil, extra	60ml/2fl oz	¼ cup
Lemon, juiced	½	½

1.
Blanch vine leaves in boiling water 3-4 minutes, drain.

2.
Mix rice, onions, tomatoes, mint, salt and pepper and oil.

3.
Place some stuffing in centre of each vine leaf (rough side up) and gently roll into tight roll, tucking sides in as you roll.

4.
Place reserved tomato skins on bottom of saucepan, pile Dolmathes on top. Add water and extra oil.

5.
Place inverted saucer on top and cook covered on low-medium heat 15 minutes. Remove plate and gently toss dolmathes, add lemon juice and cook (without plate) further 15-20 minutes. Cool slightly before serving.

6.
Can be eaten warm or cold.

Rice-Stuffed Vine Leaves

EGGS WITH TOMATOES

SERVES 2

AVGA ME TOMATES

	Metric/Imp.	U.S.
Butter	50g/2oz	3 tbsp
Large tomatoes, sliced thickly	3	3
Eggs	4	4
Black olives (optional)		
Salt and pepper		

1.
Melt butter in large frypan and fry tomatoes.

2.
Make four spaces in between tomatoes in frypan and crack one egg in each space, add olives, cook until eggs have set, spooning butter over whites of eggs regularly.

3.
Sprinkle salt and pepper over tomatoes and eggs and serve with crusty bread or on toast.

Eggs with Tomatoes

ZUCCHINI OMELET

SERVES 4

AVGA ME KOLOKITHAKIA

	Metric/Imp.	U.S.
Medium zucchinis, thinly sliced	6	6
Olive oil	80ml/3fl oz	⅓ cup
Garlic cloves, crushed	2	2
Eggs, beaten	5-6	5-6
Parmesan cheese, grated	60g/2oz	½ cup
Parsley, chopped	35g/1½oz	⅓ cup
Flour	25g/1oz	3 tbsp
Salt and pepper		

1.

Place zucchini slices in colander, sprinkle with salt, stand for a few minutes to drain excess moisture.

2.

Fry zucchini in hot oil until browned, add garlic and stir.

3.

Mix eggs, cheese, parsley, flour, salt and pepper together and pour over zucchini in pan.

4.

Cover and cook until omelet sets (approximately 15 minutes).

BRAISED CAPSICUM & ONIONS

SERVES 4

PIPERIES ME KREMITHIA

	Metric/Imp.	U.S.
Large onions, halved and sliced	2	2
Olive oil	125ml/4fl oz	½ cup
Capsicums, cut into strips	3	3
Cloves garlic, crushed	2	2
Medium, ripe tomatoes, peeled, chopped	4	4
Water	185ml/6fl oz	¾ cup
Salt and pepper		

1.
Fry onions in hot oil until soft.

2.
Add capsicum and cook until soft.

3.
Add garlic, tomatoes, water, salt and pepper and cover, reduce heat and cook 30 minutes.

NOTE
This is excellent as a side dish and can be eaten hot or cold.

MACARONI WITH YOGURT & ONIONS

SERVES 2 - 3

MACARONIA ME YAOURTI KE KREMITHIA

	Metric/Imp.	U.S.
Macaroni	250g/8oz	8 oz
Butter	25g/1oz	1½ tbsp
Olive oil	80ml/3fl oz	⅓ cup
Large onion, grated	1	1
Salt and pepper		
Parmesan cheese, grated	60g/2oz	½ cup
Yogurt, natural	500g/1lb	1 lb

1.
Cook macaroni in boiling salted water, drain, keep warm.

2.
Heat butter and oil, fry onions until well browned.

3.
Place half macaroni on serving platter, spread with half fried onions and season.

4.
Sprinkle with half cheese and spread with half yogurt.

5.
Repeat, ending with cheese and serve immediately.

CAULIFLOWER PATTIES
SERVES 4 - 6

KEFTETHES APO KOUNOUPITHI

	Metric/Imp.	U.S.
Small cauliflower, cooked	½	½
Eggs	2	2
Parsley, chopped	35g/1½oz	⅓ cup
Garlic cloves, crushed	2	2
Cumin	½ tsp	½ tsp
Water	30ml/1fl oz	2 tbsp
Salt and pepper		
Flour	35g/1½oz	4 tbsp
Oil		

1.
Chop cauliflower into small pieces, add beaten eggs, parsley, garlic, cumin, water, salt and pepper and mix.

2.
Sprinkle flour gradually into mixture and mix well.

3.
Heat oil, drop tablespoonfuls into oil and fry both sides until golden brown.

4.
Serve with meat dish.

VEGETABLE STEW

SERVES 6-8

BRIAMI

	Metric/Imp.	U.S.
Large onion, halved and sliced	1	1
Garlic cloves, chopped	2	2
Olive oil	60mls/2fl oz	¼ cup
Large capsicum, sliced	1	1
Peeled, canned tomatoes with juices, chopped	400g/14oz	1⅔ cups
Large carrot, thickly sliced	1	1
Small eggplant	1	1
Water	185ml/6fl oz	¾ cup
Medium potatoes, diced	2	2
Zucchini, thickly sliced	2	2
Peas	125g/4oz	4 oz
Beans	125g/4oz	4 oz
Salt and pepper		

1.
Brown onion and garlic in hot oil.

2.
Add capsicum, cook 2 minutes until soft and add tomatoes. Cook further 2 minutes.

3.
Add carrots, eggplant and water, cook further 2 minutes.

4.
Add potatoes, zucchini, peas, beans, salt and pepper and cook 20 minutes until potatoes are cooked.

5.
Serve hot or cold.

POTATOES WITH LEMON & OREGANO

SERVES 4

PATATOULES STO FOURNO ME RIGANI

	Metric/Imp.	U.S.
Potatoes, peeled, quartered	1kg/2lb	2 lb
Garlic cloves, crushed	2	2
Lemon, juiced	1	1
Oregano	1-1½tsp	1-1½tsp
Olive oil	¼ cup	¼ cup
Water	125ml/4fl oz	½ cup
Salt and pepper		

1.
Make 2 cuts in centre of each quartered potato. Place in baking dish.

2.
Mix all other ingredients and pour over potatoes.

3.
Bake in hot oven 40 minutes, turning potatoes once and basting regularly.

MACARONI & BROAD BEANS
A LA GREQUE

MACARONIA ME KOUKIA

	Metric/Imp.	U.S.
Small shell macaroni	250g/8oz	8 oz
Broad beans, frozen	350g/12oz	12 oz
Shallots, chopped	6	6
Canned artichokes, quartered	4-6	4-6
Large red capsicum, chopped	1	1
Black olives, whole	20	20
Pine nuts (optional)		

DRESSING

Olive oil	125ml/4oz	½ cup
Chilli powder	1 tsp	1 tsp
Oregano	2 tsp	2 tsp
Wine vinegar	60ml/2fl oz	¼ cup
Garlic cloves, crushed	2	2
Small onion, finely grated	1	1
Freshly ground black pepper		
Salt		

DRESSING

Mix all ingredients together, refrigerate at least ½ hour before using.

MACARONI & BROAD BEANS

1.

Cook macaroni and beans, drain, allow to cool.

2.

Place macaroni, beans and all other ingredients in a bowl and mix.

3.

Pour dressing on top, toss and serve.

NOTE

Marinated Artichokes Page 15 can be used.

BRAISED BROAD BEANS

KOUKIA YAHNI

	Metric/Imp.	U.S.
Large onions, sliced	2	2
Olive oil	80ml/3fl oz	⅓ cup
Broad beans, frozen	500g/1lb	1 lb
Salt and pepper		
Water	250ml/8fl oz	1 cup

1.

Brown onions in oil until soft and golden brown, add broad beans and cook 3 minutes until thawed.

2.

Season, add water, cover and cook on low heat 15-20 minutes.

3.

Serve warm or cold.

PILAF RICE

SERVES 2

PILAFI

	Metric/Imp.	U.S.
Rice	250g/8oz	1 cup
Butter	25g/1oz	1½ tbsp
Salt		
Chicken stock	375ml/12fl oz	1½ cups

1.
Wash rice in cold water and rinse several times until water runs clear.

2.
Let rice stand in cold water 20 minutes — drain.

3.
Melt butter in saucepan, add well-drained rice and salt, mix and cook 2 minutes, stirring regularly.

4.
Add stock, bring to boil, reduce heat to low and simmer 15 minutes, covered.

NOTE
Do not stir rice during cooking, water can be substituted for stock to make plain fluffy rice.

SPINACH WITH RICE
SERVES 4

SPANAKORIZO

	Metric/Imp.	U.S.
Bunch spinach	1	1
Olive oil	125ml/4fl oz	½ cup
Medium onions, grated	2	2
Peeled, canned tomatoes, chopped	375g/13oz	1½ cups
Water	440ml/14fl oz	1¾ cups
Salt and pepper		
Rice, washed	185g/6oz	¾ cup

1.
Wash and chop spinach. Stand in colander to drain moisture.

2.
Heat oil, brown onion and add tomatoes with own juices. Cook 3-4 minutes.

3.
Add half spinach, stir then add other half spinach.

4.
Cover and cook on medium heat 10-15 minutes, stirring regularly.

5.
Add water, salt and pepper, cook further 15 minutes.

6.
Add rice, cover and cook until rice is tender 20-30 minutes.

7.
Serve hot or cold.

Seafood

Thalassina

Καλή όρεχη

RICE WITH CLAMS

SERVES 2-4

PILAFI ME AHIVATHES

	Metric/Imp.	U.S.
Olive oil	125ml/4fl oz	½ cup
Onion, grated	1	1
Garlic cloves, crushed	3-4	3-4
Rice	375g/12oz	1¾ cups
Peeled, canned tomatoes, finely chopped	250g/8oz	1 cup
Canned clams with juice	400g/14oz	14 oz
Salt and pepper		
Parsley, chopped	25g/1oz	3 tbsp

1.
Heat oil and saute onion and garlic until soft.

2.
Add rice and gently cook for 2 minutes then add tomatoes with own juices.

3.
Strain clams, reserve liquid and add enough water to clam liquid to make up to 750ml/ 1½pts/3 cups and pour liquid onto rice.

4.
Cover and bring to boil, reduce heat and cook until rice is tender and liquid absorbed (if rice is not cooked and liquid evaporated, add more water).

5.
Add clams, salt and pepper, parsley, stir well and heat through before serving.

STUFFED SQUID

SERVES 4 - 6

SOUPIES YEMISTES

	Metric/Imp.	U.S.
Squid	1kg/2lb	2 lb
Potatoes, sliced	4	4
Medium onion, grated	1	1
Peeled, canned tomatoes, chopped	500g/1lb	2 cups
Olive oil	125ml/4fl oz	½ cup
Salt and freshly ground black pepper		
Water	125ml/4fl oz	½ cup

STUFFING

	Metric/Imp.	U.S.
Breadcrumbs	200g/8oz	2 cups
Medium onion, grated	1	1
Ripe tomatoes, grated	2	2
Parsley, chopped	50g/2oz	½ cup
Parmesan cheese, grated	25g/1oz	¼ cup
Egg	1	1
Garlic cloves, crushed	3	3

1.
Clean squid by peeling off brown thin skin, removing head, ink bag and intestines. Rinse well and dry.

2.
Mix together all stuffing ingredients and stuff into squid.

3.
Place squid into baking pan and arrange potatoes around.

4.
Mix all other ingredients and pour over squid and potatoes.

5.
Bake in moderately hot oven for 45 minutes-1 hour. If pan juices dry out during cooking, add more water.

6.
Serve with salad or boiled chicory.

NOTE
Head (minus eyes) can be washed, chopped into small pieces and mixed with stuffing or alternatively can be washed and placed in baking dish to cook with other ingredients.

CRABS
WITH MAYONNAISE
S E R V E S 6

KAVOURI MAYONNEZA

	Metric/Imp.	U.S.
Crabs	6	6
Mayonnaise (page 37)	500ml/1pt	2½ cups
Gherkin, chopped finely	1	1
Olive oil	40ml/1fl oz	3 tbsp
Lemon juice	20ml/1fl oz	1 tbsp
Freshly ground black pepper		
Green olives, chopped	6	6

1.
Remove main shell from crab, clean, wash and dry.

2.
Remove flesh from rest of crab, place in bowl and add gherkin, oil, lemon juice, pepper, olives and 90g/3 fl oz/⅓ cup mayonnaise. Mix well.

3.
Fill each crab shell with mixture and spread mayonnaise over crab. Garnish with slices of gherkin, olives etc.

4.
Serve as an entree on a bed of lettuce.

Crabs with Mayonnaise

FISH PIQUANT

SERVES 2

PSARI TIGANITO ME XITHI

	Metric/Imp.	U.S.
Whole fish (approx. 750 g/12 oz each	2	2
Medium carrots, sliced	2	2
Stalks celery with leaves, sliced	2	2
Medium zucchini, sliced	2	2
Large onion, halved and sliced	1	1
Garlic cloves, chopped	2	2
Twigs fresh rosemary or 3-4 tsp dried	4-5	4-5
Vinegar	125ml/4fl oz	½ cup
Oil for frying		
Flour for coating		

1.
Clean and wash fish, dry and coat in flour.

2.
Fry fish on low heat until flesh flakes easily, approximately 10 minutes. Remove from heat and keep warm.

3.
Discard all but 125ml/4fl oz/½ cup oil and add all vegetables, cook until tender.

4.
Add rosemary and stir, cook further 1 minute then add vinegar.

5.
Spoon half vegetables onto a platter, place fish on top and spoon remaining vegetables and juices over fish.

Fish Piquant

BAKED FISH
WITH GARLIC

SERVES 2

PSARI STO FOURNO

	Metric/Imp.	U.S.
Whole white fish (approx 750g/12oz each)	2	2
Garlic cloves, crushed	4-6	4-6
Oregano	1 tsp	1 tsp
Parsley, chopped	50g/2oz	½ cup
Lemon, juiced	½	½
Salt and pepper		
Olive oil	20ml/½fl oz	1½ tbsp

1.
Clean and wash fish. Pat dry.

2.
Spread inside of each fish with crushed garlic, oregano, parsley, lemon juice, salt and pepper.

3.
Place each fish on sheet of foil and brush with oil, sprinkle more parsley on top and wrap in foil.

4.
Bake in moderate oven 20-30 minutes until fish is tender.

5.
Serve with Potato Salad (Page 30).

SALT COD STEW
SERVES 4 - 6

BAKALIAROS YAHNI

	Metric/Imp.	U.S.
Salted cod	1kg/2lb	2 lb
Olive oil	125g/4fl oz	½ cup
Medium onions, halved and sliced	2	2
Garlic cloves, chopped	4	4
Peeled, canned tomatoes, chopped	500g/1lb	2 cups
Tomato paste	60g/2oz	3 tbsp
Water	500ml/1pt	2½ cups
Medium potatoes, quartered	5	5
Parsley, chopped	50g/2oz	½ cup
Freshly ground black pepper		
Black olives (with stones)	20	20

1.
Soak fish overnight in cold water, change water frequently.

2.
Scrape skin and remove bones, cut into large pieces.

3.
Fry onions in oil until lightly browned, add garlic, tomatoes, tomato paste and water. Simmer for 15 minutes.

4.
Add potatoes, cook further 10 minutes.

5.
Add fish, parsley, pepper, olives and cook further 20-30 minutes until fish and potatoes are cooked.

6.
Serve with fresh crusty bread and Greek Salad (Page 24).

BRAISED FISH
WITH VEGETABLES

S E R V E S   2 - 4

PSARI YAHNI

	Metric/Imp.	U.S.
Large, peeled tomatoes, chopped	2	2
Medium carrots, sliced	2	2
Large onion, halved and sliced	1	1
Celery stalks, sliced	3	3
Zucchini, sliced	2	2
Garlic cloves, crushed	3	3
Parsley, chopped	50g/2oz	½ cup
Water	500ml/1pt	2½ cups
Salt and pepper		
Olive oil	80ml/3fl oz	⅓ cup
Large fish cutlets (approx 250g/8oz each)	4	4

1.

Place all vegetables, water, salt and pepper in large frypan without lid and cook on medium heat for 15-20 minutes until carrots are tender and little water remains.

2.

Add oil and fish, cover and simmer 15-20 minutes until fish is cooked.

FISH MAYONNAISE

SERVES 4-6

	Metric/Imp.	U.S.
Fish	1kg/2lb	2 lb
Medium potatoes, boiled and cubed	2	2
Capers	50g/2oz	2 tbsp
Gherkins, chopped	1-2	1-2
Olives, pitted and sliced	10	10
Olive oil	40ml/1½fl oz	3 tbsp
Vinegar	3 tsp	3 tsp
Salt and pepper		
Mayonnaise (page 37)	500ml/1pt	2½ cups

1.
Boil or steam fish until cooked, debone and flake.

2.
Add potatoes, capers, gherkins, olives, oil, vinegar, salt and pepper to fish with 80mls/ 3fl oz/⅓ cup mayonnaise.

3.
Mix all ingredients and place in serving dish.

4.
Spread rest of mayonnaise over fish and garnish with sliced boiled egg, olives, gherkins, carrot rings etc.

FRIED SALT COD
SERVES 4

BAKALIAROS TIGANITOS

	Metric/Imp.	U.S.
Salted cod	500g/1lb	1 lb
Eggs, beaten	2	2
Garlic cloves, crushed	2-3	2-3
Freshly ground black pepper		
Flour	50g/1½oz	¼ cup
Water	125ml/4fl oz	½ cup
Oil		

1.
Soak cod overnight in cold water, change water frequently.

2.
Remove skin and bones, flake flesh.

3.
Place fish in bowl, add eggs, garlic, pepper, flour and enough water to form thick batter.

4.
Drop tablespoonfuls of fish mixture into hot oil and fry 3-4 minutes each side, until brown and crispy.

5.
Serve with Skorthalia Sauce (Page 36).

SQUID IN WINE
SERVES 4 - 6

SOUPIES ME KRASI

	Metric/Imp.	U.S.
Squid	1kg/2lb	2 lb
Olive oil	125ml/4fl oz	½ cup
Onions, halved and sliced	2	2
Peeled, canned tomatoes, chopped	500g/1lb	2 cups
Water	125ml/4fl oz	½ cup
Salt and pepper		
Red wine	185ml/6fl oz	¾ cup

1.
Clean squid as per Stuffed Squid (Page 71).

2.
Chop squid into 2.5 cm/1" pieces and place in frypan on medium heat, cook until all moisture from squid dries out.

3.
Add oil, onions, tomatoes, water, salt and pepper and cook for 30-45 minutes until squid is almost tender.

4.
Add red wine and cook further 15 minutes.

5.
Serve with Pilaf Rice (Page 66).

PRANS WITH FETA

SERVES 4

GARITHES ME FETA

	Metric/Imp.	U.S.
Large green prawns	1kg/2lb	2 lb
Olive oil	125ml/4fl oz	½ cup
Large onion, chopped	1	1
Shallots, chopped	6	6
Garlic cloves, crushed	3	3
Peeled, canned tomatoes, chopped	800g/28oz	3½ cups
Tomato paste	30g/1oz	1½ tbsp
Parsley, chopped	35g/1½oz	⅓ cup
Oregano	1½ tsp	1½ tsp
Freshly ground black pepper		
Dry white wine	250ml/8fl oz	1 cup
Feta cheese, cubed	125g/4oz	4 oz
Parsley, chopped, extra		

1.
Peel and devein prawns, rinse in cold water, pat dry.

2.
In large frypan, heat oil and gently fry onions, shallots and garlic until soft.

3.
Add tomatoes with juices, tomato paste, parsley, oregano, pepper and wine, simmer gently 30-40 minutes until sauce is quite thick.

4.
Add prawns and feta cheese, mix well and cook further 10-15 minutes until prawns turn pink and are cooked.

5.
Sprinkle with extra chopped parsley and serve hot with crusty bread and chilled Retsina.

FRIED CALAMARI

SERVES 4 - 6

CALAMARAKIA TIGANITA

	Metric/Imp.	U.S.
Calamari (small squid)	1kg/2lb	2 lb
Salt		
Flour		
Oil		
Lemon juice		

1.
Clean calamari by peeling off brown thin skin, removing head, ink bag and intestines. Wash well.

2.
Slice hoods in 6 mm/¼" rings, sprinkle with a little salt, coat in flour and fry in hot oil until cooked—approximately 2 minutes.

3.
Serve hot sprinkled with lemon juice or with Skorthalia Sauce (Garlic Sauce Page 36); great as part of "Meze".

OPTIONAL

Squid can be cleaned as above and the hoods and heads with tentacles fried whole.

GREEK BOUILLABAISSE

SERVES 6 - 8

KAKAVIA

	Metric/Imp.	U.S.
Fish bones and heads	2kg/4lb	4 lb
Large onion, halved	1	1
Bay leaves	2	2
Parsley, chopped	35g/1½oz	⅓ cup
Water	3ltrs/6pts	13½cups
Olive oil	80ml/3oz	⅓ cup
Large onions, halved and thinly sliced	2	2
Garlic cloves, finely chopped	3	3
Peeled, canned tomatoes, chopped	800g/28oz	3½ cups
Tomato paste	1 tsp	1 tsp
Large carrots, thickly sliced	4	4
Celery stalks with leaves, thickly chopped	4	4
Salt and freshly ground black pepper		
Baby potatoes	1kg/2lb	2 lb
Mixed fish fillets and shellfish	2kg/4lb	4 lb
Lemon, juiced	½	½
Parsley, chopped, extra	4 tsp	4 tsp

1.
Rinse fish trimmings and place in large saucepan with onion, bay leaves, parsley and water. Simmer gently 1½ hours. Strain and reserve.

2.
Heat oil and gently fry onions and garlic until soft.

3.
Add tomatoes with juices, tomato paste, carrots, celery, salt, pepper and reserved stock, bring to boil, reduce heat, cover and simmer 30 minutes.

4.
Add whole peeled potatoes and cook 10 minutes.

5.
Add firmest fish fillets first and simmer 3-5 minutes, add remaining fish and shellfish (such as green prawns and green lobster tail) and simmer approximately 10 minutes until shellfish turns pink and is cooked.

6.
Add extra chopped parsley and stir.

7.
Serve in large soup bowls with hot crusty bread. Sprinkle with lemon juice if desired.

POTATO AND ANCHOVY CROQUETTES

MAKES APPROX 2 DOZ

PATATOKEFTETHES ME ANCHOUYES

	Metric/Imp.	U.S.
Potatoes, boiled, peeled and mashed	1kg/2lb	2 lb
Eggs	2	2
Shallots, finely chopped	3	3
Parsley, chopped	25g/1oz	3 tbsp
Anchovy fillets	50g/2oz	2 oz
Onion, grated	1	1
Salt and freshly ground black pepper		
Breadcrumbs	50g/2oz	½ cup
Oil		

1.

Mix all ingredients together except breadcrumbs and oil.

2.

Shape into patties or croquettes, roll in breadcrumbs.

3.

Fry in hot oil 4-5 minutes each side.

Poultry & Game

Poulerika Ke Kynigika

Καλή όρεχη

CHICKEN RISSOLES
SERVES 2 - 4

KEFTETHES APO KOTA

	Metric/Imp.	U.S.
Minced raw chicken	500g/1lb	1 lb
Shallots, finely chopped	2	2
Small onion, grated	1	1
Small potato, finely grated	1	1
Parsley, chopped	25g/1oz	3 tbsp
Dried thyme	1 tsp	1 tsp
Oregano	½ tsp	½ tsp
Eggs, beaten	2	2
Salt and pepper		
Breadcrumbs	25g/1oz	3 tbsp
Breadcrumbs, extra		
Oil		

1.
Mix all ingredients except extra breadcrumbs and oil.

2.
Shape into balls and coat well in extra breadcrumbs.

3.
Fry in hot oil until golden brown.

BRAISED CHICKEN WITH OKRA
SERVES 4 - 6

BAMIES ME KOTA

	Metric/Imp.	U.S.
Chicken pieces	1.5kg/3lb	3 lb
Olive oil	4 tsp	4 tsp
Butter or margarine	50g/2oz	3 tbsp
Large onion, chopped	1	1
Garlic cloves, chopped	2	2
Peeled, canned tomatoes, chopped	500g/1lb	2 cups
Tomato paste	30g/1oz	1½ tbsp
Red wine	125ml/4fl oz	½ cup
Bay leaves	2	2
Parsley, chopped	15g/½oz	1½ tbsp
Cinnamon stick	1	1
Water	125ml/4fl oz	½ cup
Salt and pepper		
Canned okra, drained	800g/28oz	28 oz

1.
Remove excess fat from chicken, wash and pat dry.

2.
Heat oil and butter in heavy saucepan, add chicken pieces and brown a few at a time. Remove.

3.
Add onion and garlic, cook until onion is tender.

4.
Add tomatoes with juices and other ingredients except okra and chicken pieces and cook for 10 minutes.

5.
Add chicken pieces, cover and cook further 30-45 minutes until chicken is tender. Add more water if juices dry out.

6.
Add drained okra and cook further 10-15 minutes.

7.
Serve hot wih Pilaf Rice (Page 66).

SPICY BRAISED CHICKEN

S E R V E S   4 - 6

KOTOPOULO KAPAMA

	Metric/Imp.	U.S.
Chicken pieces	2kg/4lb	4 lb
Olive oil	60ml/2fl oz	¼ cup
Butter	25g/1oz	1½ tbsp
Onions, chopped	2	2
Garlic cloves, chopped	2	2
Lemon, juiced	1	1
Ground cloves	¼ tsp	¼ tsp
Cinnamon sticks	2	2
Water	125ml/4fl oz	½ cup
Peeled, canned tomatoes, including liquid	800g/28oz	3½ cups
Tomato paste	30g/1oz	1½ tbsp
White wine	125ml/4fl oz	½ cup
Salt and pepper		
Black olives	12-15	12-15

1.
Remove excess fat from chicken, wash and pat dry.

2.
Heat oil and butter in large saucepan and saute chicken pieces a few at a time, remove and set aside.

3.
Add onion and garlic to saucepan and saute until onion is soft.

4.
Add all other ingredients except olives and chicken. Bring to boil, reduce heat and simmer 30 minutes.

5.
Return chicken to pot and simmer further 45 minutes until chicken is cooked.

6.
Add olives, remove cinnamon sticks and serve with Pilaf Rice (Page 66).

CHICKEN WITH WHITE LEMON SAUCE

SERVES 4

KOTOPOULO LEMONATO

	Metric/Imp.	U.S.
Cloves	3	3
Onions	3	3
Chicken	1½ kg/3 lb	
Celery stalks, sliced	2	2
Carrots, sliced	3	3
Salt and pepper		
Water		
Flour	50g/1½oz	¼ cup
Egg yolks	2	2
Lemons, juiced	1-1½	1-1½

1.
Insert 1 clove into each onion.

2.
Place chicken, onions, celery, carrots, salt and pepper into saucepan, cover with water, cook until chicken is tender, approximately 40 minutes.

3.
Remove chicken and cloves from saucepan. Discard cloves, skin and debone chicken, cut into pieces.

4.
Mix flour with a little stock, return chicken to saucepan and add flour mixture. Stir until sauce begins to thicken, remove from heat, cool slightly.

5.
Beat eggs with lemon juice and add to chicken, stir until sauce thickens.

6.
Serve on a bed of rice.

CHICKEN WITH GARLIC & LEMON

SERVES 4 - 6

KOTOPOULO LEMONATO ME SKORTHO

	Metric/Imp.	U.S.
Chicken pieces	2kg/4lb	4 lb
Flour		
Butter, melted	50g/2oz	3 tbsp

MARINADE

Olive oil	80ml/3fl oz	⅓ cup
Lemons, juice and rind	2	2
Oregano	1½ tsp	1½ tsp
Garlic cloves, crushed	3	3
Salt and pepper		

1.
Mix all marinade ingredients together and chill for at least 1 hour.

2.
Coat chicken pieces in flour and place in baking dish skin side down in one layer.

3.
Pour melted butter over chicken and bake in moderately hot oven for 30 minutes.

4.
Turn chicken over, pour marinade over and cook a further 40 minutes.

CHICKEN LIVERS
IN WINE SAUCE
SERVES 4

SIKOTAKIA TIS KOTAS
ME KRASSI

	Metric/Imp.	U.S.
Butter	125g/4oz	½ cup
Chicken livers, trimmed	1kg/2lb	2 lb
Medium onions, chopped	3	3
Garlic cloves, chopped	3	3
Tomato paste	125g/4oz	½ cup
Bay leaves	2	2
Wine	125ml/4fl oz	½ cup
Water	625ml/1¼pts	3 cups
Salt and pepper		

1.
Heat butter in heavy saucepan and fry chicken livers a few at a time. Remove from heat.

2.
Add onions and garlic, cook until tender. Add tomato paste, stir and cook further 2 minutes.

3.
Add livers, bayleaves, wine, water, salt and pepper and cook on medium heat 30-45 minutes.

4.
Serve on Pilaf Rice (Page 66) or macaroni.

BAKED CHICKEN

S E R V E S   4

KOTOPOULO STO FOURNO

	Metric/Imp.	U.S.
Chicken	1.5kg/3lb	3 lb
Garlic cloves, crushed	1-2	1-2
Oregano	1½ tsp	1½ tsp
Salt and pepper		
Lemon, juiced	1	1
Water	500m/1pt	2½ cups
Butter	25g/1oz	1½ tbsp
Small orange, juiced	1	1

1.

Place chicken, garlic, oregano, salt, pepper, lemon juice and water in baking dish.

2.

Dob chicken with butter and place in hot oven. Cook 20-30 minutes, turn chicken and pour half orange juice over chicken.

3.

Cook further 20 minutes or until browned.

4.

Turn chicken, pour rest of orange juice over and cook until browned and chicken cooked— approximately 20-30 minutes.

5.

Baste chicken regularly with pan juices during cooking.

6.

Vegetables such as potatoes and pumpkin can be added to pan half way through cooking. Baste regularly.

STUFFED TURKEY

SERVES 6-8

GHALLOS YEMISTOS

	Metric/Imp.	U.S.
Rice	250g/8oz	1¼ cups
Chicken livers	500g/1lb	1 lb
Oil	80ml/3fl oz	⅓ cup
Turkey liver		
Onion, chopped	1	1
Sultanas	100g/3oz	½ cup
Pine nuts	125g/4oz	½ cup
Cinnamon	1 tsp	1 tsp
Salt and pepper		
Water	125ml/4fl oz	½ cup
Turkey	3.5kg/7lb	7 lb
Butter, melted	50g/2oz	3 tbsp
Water, extra	125ml/4fl oz	½ cup
Lemon, juiced	1	1
Orange, juiced	1	1

1.
Soak rice in boiling water for 5 minutes and drain.

2.
Wash livers, fry in hot oil until browned.

3.
Remove from heat, chop and return to pan with onion and saute 2-3 minutes.

4.
Add rice and fry 5 minutes, stirring constantly.

5.
Add sultanas, pine nuts, cinnamon, salt, pepper and water and cook 10 minutes until rice is half cooked—add more water if mixture dries out.

6.
Stuff turkey with above mixture and secure opening.

7.
Place turkey on baking tray and pour butter, extra water, lemon and orange juice over and sprinkle with pepper and salt.

8.
Bake in moderate oven 1½-2 hours or until turkey is cooked and golden brown. Baste regularly. If pan juices dry out add more water.

RABBIT STEW WITH EGG & LEMON SAUCE

SERVES 4-6

KOUNELI AVGOLEMONO

	Metric/Imp.	U.S.
Rabbit	1½kg/3lb	3lb
Olive oil	80ml/3fl oz	⅓ cup
Onion, grated	1	1
Celery stalks with leaves, chopped	4	4
Carrots, sliced	3	3
Small onions	3	3
Bay leaves	2	2
Salt and pepper		
Water		
Flour	25g/1oz	3 tbsp
Egg yolks	2	2
Lemons, juiced	1½	1½

1.
Joint rabbit, boil in salted water 10 minutes, drain.

2.
Heat oil in heavy-based saucepan and brown rabbit.

3.
Add grated onion, saute 2 minutes.

4.
Add celery, carrots, small onions, bay leaves, salt and pepper, cover with water and cook on medium heat 45 minutes or until rabbit is tender.

5.
Mix flour with a little rabbit stock, add to stew and stir.

6.
Remove from heat and cool slightly.

7.
Beat egg yolks, mix with lemon juice, add to casserole and heat through.

Meat

Kreata

Καλή όρεχη

BEEF WITH TOMATOES
& OREGANO

SERVES 4

KREAS STO FOURNO
ME RIGANI

	Metric/Imp.	U.S.
Lean beef, cut into 4	1kg/2lb	2 lb
Large onions, grated	2	2
Garlic cloves, finely grated	4	4
Peeled, canned tomatoes, chopped	500g/1lb	2 cups
Oregano	2 tsp	2 tsp
Salt and freshly ground black pepper		
Olive oil	60ml/2fl oz	¼ cup
Water	750ml/1½pts	3 cups

1.

Place beef in large baking dish in one layer and spread onion, garlic and tomatoes on top, sprinkle with oregano.

2.

Season with salt and pepper, pour oil and water on top.

3.

Bake in moderately hot oven for 1-1½ hours, until meat is tender and sauce is thick.

4.

Baste meat regularly, juices should not dry out—add more water during cooking if they do.

5.

Serve with rice or roast potatoes and salad.

MEAT BALLS (1)

SERVES 4 - 6
approx. 40 balls

KEFTETHES

	Metric/Imp.	U.S.
Beef or lamb mince	1kg/2lb	2 lb
Large onion, grated	1	1
Garlic cloves, crushed	2	2
Eggs, lightly beaten	2	2
Parsley chopped	35g/1½oz	⅓ cup
Large potato, grated	1	1
Olive oil	30ml/1fl oz	2 tbsp
Oregano	1 tsp	1 tsp
Salt and pepper		
Flour for coating		
Oil for frying		

1.
Mix all ingredients well.

2.
Roll into walnut-sized balls and coat in flour.

3.
Fry in hot oil until well browned.

4.
Serve with Cauliflower Salad (Page 32) and fried potatoes.

VARIATION
Add leftover meat balls to a rich red parsley sauce and served on a bed of rice or with chunky fried potatoes. Grate 1 small onion and 1 garlic clove and brown in a little oil. Add 90g/3oz/⅓ cup tomato paste, 50g/2oz/½ cup parsley, 125ml/4fl oz/½ cup red wine and 375ml/12fl oz/1½ cups water, salt and pepper. Simmer 20 minutes, add meat balls, heat through and serve.

MEAT BALLS (II)

SERVES 4
approx 20 balls

KEFTETHES (II)

	Metric/Imp.	U.S.
Slices bread	3	3
Mince beef or lamb	500g/1lb	1 lb
Eggs	2	2
Flour	15g/½oz	1½ tbsp
Oregano	1 tsp	1 tsp
Large onion, grated	1	1
Garlic cloves, crushed	2	2
Olive oil	20ml/½fl oz	1½ tbsp
Salt and pepper		
Flour		
Oil		

1.
Soak bread in water for 10 minutes. Drain, squeeze bread dry and rub into crumbs.

2.
Mix bread and other ingredients together and form into balls.

3.
Coat in flour and fry in hot oil until golden brown, approximately 3-4 minutes each side.

4.
Serve hot or cold.

NOTE
Shape half the normal size for parties and serve cold.

POT ROAST
SERVES 4 - 6

KREAS KRASATO

	Metric/Imp.	U.S.
Piece of beef	1½kg/3lb	3 lb
Garlic cloves	2	2
Olive oil	60ml/2fl oz	¼ cup
Butter	25g/1oz	1½ tbsp
Large onion, chopped	1	1
Garlic cloves, crushed (extra)	2	2
Red wine	250ml/8fl oz	1 cup
Water	500ml/1pt	2½ cups
Bay leaves	2	2
Salt and freshly ground black pepper		

1.
Make two small incisions in beef, insert a garlic clove in each.

2.
Heat oil and butter in large saucepan, add meat and brown.

3.
Add onion and extra garlic, cook until onion is soft.

4.
Add red wine, water, bayleaves, salt and pepper and reduce heat, cover and simmer for 1½-2 hours until meat is tender.

5.
Serve beef with sauce spooned over or thicken sauce with 25g/1 oz/2 tbsp flour. Small round potatoes can be peeled, halved and fried then dropped into sauce. Let stand for 5 minutes until potatoes have absorbed some sauce before serving.

BEEF AND ZUCCHINI IN EGG AND LEMON SAUCE

SERVES 2-4

KOLOKITHAKIA ME KREAS AVGOLEMONO

	Metric/Imp.	U.S.
Olive oil	125ml/4fl oz	½ cup
Zucchini, thickly sliced	1kg/2lb	2 lb
Lean beef, cubed	500g/1lb	1 lb
Onions, grated	2	2
Garlic clove, crushed	1	1
Water	500ml/1pt	2½ cups
Salt and pepper		
Egg yolks	2	2
Lemon, juiced	1	1

1.

Heat oil in saucepan, saute zucchini, remove from pan and set aside.

2.

Add meat, onion and garlic, saute until meat is browned.

3.

Add water, salt and pepper, cover and simmer until meat is almost tender (add more water if needed).

4.

Add zucchini and cook further 10-15 minutes until meat is tender, remove from heat and cool.

5.

Beat egg yolks with lemon juice, mix in a little meat and zucchini stock and pour into saucepan.

6.

Stir and return to heat and cook for a few minutes until sauce thickens.

7.

Pour over meat and serve with Pilaf Rice (Page 66).

MEAT LOAF
SERVES 4-6

KIMA ROULO

	Metric/Imp.	U.S.
Mince steak	1kg/2lb	2 lb
Onion, grated	1	1
Garlic cloves, crushed	2	2
Eggs	2	2
Parsley, chopped	25g/1oz	3 tbsp
Breadcrumbs	25g/1oz	¼ cup
Olive oil	40ml/1½fl oz	3 tbsp
Oregano	1 tsp	1 tsp
Salt and pepper		
Extra breadcrumbs		

FILLING

	Metric/Imp.	U.S.
Parsley	50g/2oz	½ cup
Parmesan cheese, grated	25g/1oz	¼ cup
Hard boiled eggs, shelled	4-5	4-5
Olives, pitted and halved	10	10
Extra breadcrumbs		
Water	375ml/12fl oz	1½ cups
Oil	40ml/1½fl oz	3 tbsp

1.
Mix meat and other ingredients together and flatten into oblong shape.

2.
Place filling in centre by sprinkling parsley and cheese over meat, place eggs and olives on top. Carefully roll meat over filling to make smooth roll. Sprinkle with extra breadcrumbs.

3.
Place in baking dish with water and oil and bake in moderately hot oven 1-1½ hours, basting regularly.

4.
Potatoes can be added halfway through cooking time. Serve with Zucchini Salad (Page 26).

MINCE MEAT SAUCE

SERVES 4-6

KIMA SALTSA

	Metric/Imp.	U.S.
Olive oil	60ml/2fl oz	¼ cup
Mince steak	1kg/2lb	2 lb
Large onions, grated	2	2
Garlic cloves, crushed	2	2
Tomato paste	250g/8oz	1 cup
Sugar	1 tsp	1 tsp
Bay leaves	2	2
Salt and pepper		
Water	750ml/1½pts	3½ cups
Red wine	250ml/8fl oz	1 cup

1.
Heat oil, brown meat, add onions and garlic, saute.

2.
Add tomato paste, stir and add sugar, cook 1-2 minutes.

3.
Add bay leaves, salt, pepper and water, cook 45 minutes—1 hour.

4.
Add wine, continue to cook until meat is tender and sauce thick, approximately half an hour.

5.
Serve over macaroni or spaghetti.

CORNED BEEF PATTIES

SERVES 4

	Metric/Imp.	U.S.
Slices bread	3	3
Corned beef, canned	425g/15oz	15 oz
Large onion, grated	1	1
Garlic clove, grated	1	1
Egg	1	1
Parsley, chopped	25g/1oz	¼ cup
Ground cumin	1 tsp	1 tsp
Salt and pepper		
Flour		
Oil		

1.
Soak bread in water for 10 minutes, squeeze dry and crumble.

2.
Mash corned beef with fork and add all other ingredients.

3.
Mix well and shape into balls, coat in flour and fry in hot oil until golden brown.

SKEWERED LAMB

SERVES 6-8

SOUVLAKIA

	Metric/Imp.	U.S.
Leg of lamb, boned	1½-2kg	3-4 lb
Oregano	2 tsp	2 tsp
Lemons, juiced	2	2
Olive oil	125ml/4fl oz	½ cup
Garlic cloves, crushed	3	3
Salt and pepper		

1.
Cut meat into 2.5 cm/1" cubes and place in marinating dish.

2.
Mix all other ingredients and pour over meat.

3.
Cover and refrigerate overnight, stirring occasionally.

4.
Thread onto metal or bamboo skewers.

5.
Cook under medium grill/broil or barbecue, turning and basting regularly with marinade, for approximately 20 minutes.

6.
Serve with fried potatoes and salad.

VARIATION
Pieces of onion and capsicum can be placed between lamb pieces.

NOTE
If using bamboo skewers, soak overnight in oil to prevent burning.

Skewered Lamb

BEEF ROLLS IN RED SAUCE

SERVES 4 - 6

KREAS ROULO ME SALTSA

	Metric/Imp.	U.S.
Beef sliced in 5 pieces	1kg/2lb	2 lb
Oil	60ml/2fl oz	¼ cup
Butter	35g/1½oz	2 tbsp
Medium onions, grated	2	2
Garlic cloves, grated	2	2
Tomato paste	90g/3oz	⅓ cup
Peeled, canned tomatoes, finely chopped	400g/14oz	1⅔ cups
Sugar	½ tsp	½ tsp
Salt and pepper		
Water	500ml/1pt	2½ cups
Red wine	80ml/3fl oz	⅓ cup

STUFFING

Parsley, chopped	100g/4oz	1 cup
Garlic cloves, crushed	6-8	6-8
Parmesan or Romano cheese, cubed	125g/4oz	4 oz
Parmesan cheese, grated	25g/1oz	2 tbsp
Hard boiled eggs, halved	5	5
Salt and pepper		

1.
Prepare meat by slicing each piece in half lengthways to make one large very thin slice.

2.
Along centre of each slice of meat (lengthways) place some parsley, garlic, cheese cubes, grated cheese and 2 halves of egg. Sprinkle with salt and pepper.

3.
Gently roll to form a long roll and secure by winding doubled sewing cotton around each roll.

4.
In heavy saucepan heat oil and butter and add meat rolls.

5.
Brown rolls and add onion and garlic, cook until soft.

6.
Add tomato paste, peeled tomatoes with juices and sugar, stir, cook 1-2 minutes.

7.
Add salt, pepper, water and wine. Bring to boil and reduce heat. Cook on medium heat for approximately 1 hour 45 minutes.

8.
Remove cotton and serve by thickly slicing rolls and pouring sauce over meat.

Beef Rolls in Red Sauce

FRIED SAUSAGES

SERVES 4

SOUZOUKAKIA TIGANITA

	Metric/Imp.	U.S.
Mince steak	500g/1lb	1 lb
Cumin	1 tsp	1 tsp
Onion, grated	1	1
Dry breadcrumbs	50g/2oz	½ cup
Egg	1	1
Salt and pepper		
Flour for coating		
Oil for frying		

1.
Mix all ingredients together and shape into small sausages.

2.
Coat sausages with flour and fry in hot oil for 3-4 minutes each side until well browned.

3.
Serve with salad and fried potatoes.

MEAT AND PEAS IN RED SAUCE

SERVES 4

KREAS SALTSA ME PIZELIA

	Metric/Imp.	U.S.
Olive oil	60ml/2fl oz	¼ cup
Butter	25g/1oz	1½ tbsp
Lamb or beef, cubed	1kg/2lb	2 lb
Large onion, chopped	1	1
Garlic cloves, chopped	2	2
Tomato paste	150g/5oz	⅔ cup
Water	500ml/1pt	2½ cups
Salt and pepper		
Peas	500g/1lb	1 lb

1.
Heat oil and butter in large saucepan, add meat and brown.

2.
Add onion and garlic, cook until onion is tender.

3.
Add tomato paste, water, salt and pepper. Cover, reduce heat and simmer approximately 1 hour, until meat is almost cooked.

4.
Add peas, cover and cook until meat and peas are tender, add more water if liquid dries out.

5.
Serve over Pilaf Rice (Page 66).

VARIATION
Beans or spinach can be substituted for the peas.

LAMB AND POTATO CASSEROLE

SERVES 4

ARNI ME PATATES KE TOMATES

	Metric/Imp.	U.S.
Lamb chops	1½kg/3lb	3 lb
Large potatoes, sliced	3	3
Medium onions, sliced	2	2
Large ripe tomatoes, sliced	3	3
Tomato paste	30g/1oz	1½tbsp
Water	125ml/4fl oz	½ cup
Red wine	80ml/3fl oz	⅓ cup
Cinnamon	1 tsp	1 tsp
Salt		
Freshly ground black pepper		

1.
Place alternate layers of chops, potatoes, onion and tomatoes in deep baking dish, finishing with layer of tomatoes.

2.
Mix tomato paste, water, wine, cinnamon, salt and pepper together, pour over meat and vegetables.

3.
Cover and cook in moderately hot oven for 1¼ hours.

4.
Remove lid and cook further 30 minutes or until meat is tender.

5.
Serve with salad and fresh crusty bread.

VARIATION

a. 1 teaspoon oregano can be substituted for cinnamon.

b. Prepare dish omitting meat and wine, cook for 1 hour.

NOTE

This casserole tastes best if prepared one day ahead.

ROAST LEG OF LAMB

SERVES 4-6

ARNI PSITO

	Metric/Imp.	U.S.
Leg of lamb	1½kg/3lb	3 lb
Garlic cloves, in slivers	3	3
Lemons, juiced	2	2
Oregano	3 tsp	3 tsp
Garlic clove, crushed	1	1
Butter	25g/1oz	1½ tbsp
Water	375ml/12fl oz	1½ cups
Salt and pepper		

1.
Trim excess fat from meat.

2.
Make three incisions in lamb, insert garlic slivers.

3.
Place lamb in baking dish, pour over lemon juice, sprinkle with oregano and crushed garlic and dob with butter.

4.
Add water, season to taste and bake in moderately hot oven for 1½-2 hours. Baste regularly and turn lamb over twice during cooking. If juices in pan dry out, add more water.

NOTE

Whole baby potatoes can be added to the pan 40 minutes before end of cooking time. Baste potatoes regularly.

GRILLED LAMB CHOPS
SERVES 4

PAITHAKIA STI SKARA

	Metric/Imp.	U.S.
Lamb chops	1kg/2lb	2 lb
Garlic cloves, crushed	3	3
Oregano	2 tsp	2 tsp
Lemons, juiced	2	2
Salt and pepper		
Olive oil	60ml/2fl oz	¼ cup

1.
Place chops in deep dish to marinate.

2.
Mix other ingredients together and pour over lamb.

3.
Cover, place in refrigerator and marinate for 3 hours (preferrably overnight) turning occasionally.

4.
Grill/broil, basting with any remaining marinade.

VARIATION

Prepare marinade and refrigerate in glass jar with lid (lasts for weeks). Use marinade to brush over lamb chops during grilling/broiling.

NOTE

These are delicious for barbecues.

BAKED SAUSAGES WITH TOMATO
SERVES 4

SOUZOUKAKIA STO FOURNO

	Metric/Imp.	U.S.
Mince steak	500g/1lb	1 lb
Medium onion, grated	1	1
Egg	1	1
Fresh mint, chopped	2 tsp	2 tsp
Salt and pepper		
Slices bread, (soak, squeeze dry and rub into crumbs)	3	3

TOPPING

	Metric/Imp.	U.S.
Peeled, canned tomatoes, chopped with juice	500g/1lb	2 cups
Onion, grated	1	1
Water	125ml/4fl oz	½ cup
Olive oil	80ml/3fl oz	⅓ cup
Salt and pepper		

1.
Mix mince and other ingredients together.

2.
Shape into small sausage shapes and place in baking dish in single layer.

3.
Mix topping ingredients together and pour over sausages.

4.
Bake in moderate-hot oven 1-1¼ hours until cooked.

5.
Serve with mashed potatoes and string beans with olive oil and lemon dressing.

BAKED LAMB
WITH NOODLES

SERVES 6 - 8

YIOUVETSI

	Metric/Imp.	U.S.
Leg lamb	2kg/4lb	4 lb
Garlic clove, cut into 4 slivers	1	1
Oil	40ml/1fl oz	3 tbsp
Butter	25g/1oz	1½ tbsp
Large onions, grated	2	2
Garlic cloves, grated	2	2
Peeled, canned tomatoes, chopped	650g/1½lbs	3 cups
Cinnamon	2 tsp	2 tsp
Water	250ml/8fl oz	1 cup
Salt and pepper		
Risone pasta	500g/1lb	1 lb
Water, extra	1¾ltrs/3pts	7 cups
Parmesan cheese, grated		

1.
Make 4 incisions in lamb and insert garlic slivers.

2.
Place lamb in large baking dish, add oil, butter, onions, garlic, tomatoes, cinnamon, water, salt and pepper. Baste lamb with tomato mixture.

3.
Bake in hot oven 2-2½ hours, turning lamb occasionally and basting with pan juices. Remove lamb from pan and keep warm.

4.
Add risone and extra water to pan, stir.

5.
Return to oven and bake, stirring regularly until risone is cooked—approximately 1 hour. If risone dries out add more water.

6.
Serve slices of lamb with risone sprinkled with grated parmesan cheese.

LAMBS FRY
WITH VINEGAR

SERVES 2-4

SIKOTAKI XITHATO

	Metric/Imp.	U.S.
Lambs fry, sliced	500g/1lb	1 lb
Flour		
Oil	500ml/1pt	2½ cups
Rosemary leaves	3 tsp	3 tsp
Vinegar	80ml/3fl oz	⅓ cup

1.
Coat lambs fry with flour, fry in hot oil until tender.

2.
Remove from frypan, set aside.

3.
Discard all but 80ml/3fl oz/⅓ cup oil and return to heat, add rosemary and mix well. Cook 1 minute.

4.
Remove from heat, add vinegar and stir.

5.
Return lambs fry to pan, coat well with pan juices and heat through.

6.
Serve with mashed potato and green vegetable salad.

BRAIN PATTIES
SERVES 4-6

KEFTETHES APO MIALA

	Metric/Imp.	U.S.
Brains	6	6
Eggs	3	3
Water	40ml/1½fl oz	3 tbsp
Flour	50g/1½oz	¼ cup
Salt and pepper		
Oil for frying		

1.

Soak brains in water for 30 minutes and remove thin layer of skin.

2.

Boil brains in water for 10-15 minutes, drain and cool.

3.

Beat eggs, water and flour together to form batter.

4.

Chop brains into small pieces, add to batter with salt and pepper.

5.

Heat oil and fry tablespoonfuls of mixture for 3-4 minutes each side, until golden brown.

6.

Serve with green vegetables.

TRIPE
IN TOMATO SAUCE
SERVES 2 - 4

TRIPA ME SALTSA

	Metric/Imp.	U.S.
Tripe, washed and sliced into strips	1kg/2lb	2 lb
Olive oil	80ml/3fl oz	⅓ cup
Large onions, sliced	3	3
Peeled, canned tomatoes, chopped	500g/1lb	2 cups
Tomato paste	90g/3oz	⅓ cup
Parsley, chopped	75g/3oz	¾ cup
Bay leaf	1	1
Salt and freshly ground black pepper		
Water	500ml/1pt	2½ cups
Parmesan or kefalotiri cheese, grated		

1.
Cook tripe on medium heat until all moisture evaporates.

2.
Add oil and onions, fry until onions are soft.

3.
Add tomatoes, tomato paste, parsley, bay leaf, salt, pepper and water and simmer until tripe is cooked and sauce thickens, 1-1½ hours.

4.
Serve topped with grated cheese on macaroni.

PORK WITH CELERY

SERVES 4 - 6

HIRINO ME SELINO

	Metric/Imp.	U.S.
Bunches celery	1½	1½
Butter	25g/1oz	1½tbsp
Olive oil	125ml/4fl oz	½ cup
Pork chops	1kg/2lb	2 lb
Medium onions, chopped	2	2
Salt and pepper		
Water		
Flour	25g/1oz	3 tbsp
Eggs	2	2
Lemons, juiced	1	1½

1.
Separate stalks and remove string from celery — do not remove leaves — wash and dry well. Cut into 5cm/2" pieces.

2.
Heat butter and oil in large saucepan, brown chops and remove from pan.

3.
Add onions and cook until soft.

4.
Return chops to pan, add salt and pepper, cover with water and cook 30-40 minutes until meat is almost cooked.

5.
Add celery, cook further 30 minutes until meat and celery are tender. Celery should not be over-cooked.

6.
Mix flour with some celery stock, pour into meat and stir gently until mixture starts to thicken.

7.
Remove from heat and cool slightly.

8.
Beat eggs with lemon juice and add to pork.

9.
Return to heat, stirring gently until heated through, do not boil. Serve with crusty bread.

ROAST PORK
SERVES 6-8

HIRINO PSITO

	Metric/Imp.	U.S.
Leg of pork	2-2½kg/4-5lbs	4-5 lbs
Olive oil	40ml/1½fl oz	3 tbsp
Salt and pepper		
Lemons, juiced	2	2
Water	125ml/4fl oz	½ cup
Can beer	1	1

1.
Cut a few slits across leg of pork and rub with oil, salt and pepper.

2.
Place pork in roasting pan with water and pour lemon juice over pork.

3.
Bake in hot oven. After half an hour, pour ⅓ can of beer over pork, repeat this twice more during cooking. Cook pork until tender (approximately 2-2½ hours) basting regularly with pan juices.

Mince Dishes

Kimathes

Καλή όρεχη

BAKED STUFFED CABBAGE ROLLS

S E R V E S   4 - 6

LAHANO DOLMATHES STO FOURNO

1 medium cabbage		

STUFFING

	Metric/Imp.	U.S.
Olive oil	80ml/3fl oz	⅓ cup
Mince steak	500g/1lb	1 lb
Pork mince	500g/1lb	1 lb
Onions, grated	2	2
Garlic cloves, crushed	2	2
Peeled, canned tomatoes, chopped	500g/1lb	2 cups
Salt and pepper		
Parsley, chopped	50g/2oz	½ cup
Eggs, beaten	3	3
Parmesan cheese, grated	25g/1oz	¼ cup
Cooked rice	125g/4oz	½ cup

SAUCE

	Metric/Imp.	U.S.
Olive oil	60ml/2fl oz	¼ cup
Onions, halved and sliced	3	3
Garlic cloves, crushed	2	2
Peeled, canned tomatoes, chopped	500g/1lb	2 cups
Tomato paste	90g/3oz	⅓ cup
Water	125ml/4fl oz	½ cup
Salt and pepper		

METHOD

1.

Blanch cabbage in salted, boiling water for 5 minutes—drain and separate leaves. Remove thick base from leaves.

2.

Prepare stuffing—heat oil and brown minces, add onion and garlic, saute until onion is soft.

3.

Add tomatoes, salt and pepper, cook 20 minutes then remove from heat and cool.

4.

Add parsley, egg, cheese and rice, mix well.

5.

Place some stuffing on each cabbage leaf and roll into fairly large rolls and place side by side in baking dish.

6.

Pour sauce over rolls and bake in moderate oven for 1 hour.

SAUCE

1.

Heat oil, fry onions and garlic.

2.

Add tomatoes, tomato paste, water, salt and pepper.

Cook approximately 10 minutes until sauce starts to thicken.

Baked Stuffed Cabbage Rolls

EGGPLANT RISSOLES
SERVES 6

KEFTETHES APO MELINTZANA

	Metric/Imp.	U.S.
Eggplant 600g/1¼lb	1	1
Medium onions, sliced	2	2
Water	750ml/1½pts	3 cups
Fine mince steak	500g/1lb	1 lb
Eggs	2	2
Breadcrumbs	50g/2oz	½ cup
Garlic clove, crushed	1	1
Oregano	1 tsp	1 tsp
Mint	1 tsp	1 tsp
Salt and pepper		

1.

Cook eggplant and onions in water approximately 40 minutes until soft. Drain well—chop.

2.

Mix eggplant and onions with other ingredients and form into balls.

3.

Coat in extra breadcrumbs and fry in hot oil until golden brown—approximately 3 minutes each side.

Moussaka (see p. 124)

STUFFED VINE LEAF ROLLS

SERVES 6-8

DOLMATHAKIA

	Metric/Imp.	U.S.
Rice	*180g/5oz*	*¾ cup*
Vine leaves	*500g/1lb*	*1 lb*
Medium tomatoes, grated	3	3
Mince steak	*1kg/2lb*	*2 lb*
Large onion, grated	1	1
Butter, melted	*50g/2oz*	*3 tbsp*
Olive oil	*40ml/1½fl oz*	*3 tbsp*
Salt and pepper		
Water	*500ml/1pt*	*2½ cups*
Lemons, juiced	*1-1½*	*1-1½*
Butter, extra	*50g/2oz*	*3 tbsp*

1.

Wash rice, soak in hot water 10 minutes, drain well.

2.

Blanch vine leaves in boiling water 5 minutes, drain.

3.

Line bottom of large saucepan with tomato skins (outer skin side up).

4.

Mix together mince, rice, onions, tomatoes, melted butter, oil, salt and pepper.

5.

Cut stem off each vine leaf and place small spoonfuls of filling in centre of each leaf on rough side.

6.

Fold over sides and roll up tightly to make a small roll. Repeat until all filling and vine leaves are used, the larger leaves can be cut into two.

7.

Pack Dolmathakia on top of tomato skins in saucepan in layers and add water, lemon juice and extra butter.

8.

Place inverted saucer on top of Dolmathakia to prevent them from opening during cooking. Cover saucepan, bring to boil and reduce heat and simmer 45 minutes-1 hour until Dolmathakia are cooked.

9.

Remove from saucepan very gently and serve hot with some juices poured over or with Avgolemono Sauce (Page 38).

NOTE

Add more water if liquid dries out during cooking. Dolmathakia should be moist when served and taste better and are easier to handle if left in saucepan for 2 hours after cooking and are then reheated gently before serving.

STUFFED ZUCCHINI
WITH EGG
& LEMON SAUCE

SERVES 4 - 6

KOLOKITHAKIA YEMISTA AVGOLEMONO

	Metric/Imp.	U.S.
Medium sized zucchini	10-12	10-12
Mince steak	375g/12oz	12 oz
Rice, washed and drained	125g/4oz	½ cup
Large tomatoes, grated	3	3
Large onion, grated	1	1
Garlic cloves, grated	2	2
Parsley, chopped	25g/1oz	¼ cup
Butter	50g/2oz	3 tbsp
Olive oil	60ml/2fl oz	¼ cup
Salt and pepper		
Water	1¼ ltrs/2¼ pts	6 cups
Olive oil, extra	60ml/2fl oz	¼ cup

1.
Wash zucchini and slightly scrape some skin off each one. Cut off the stem and gently scoop out most of the flesh.

2.
With a sharp knife cut a slit across the bottom of zucchini (this aids cooking process).

3.
Combine mince with all ingredients except water and extra oil. Mix well and stuff zucchini tightly.

4.
Place zucchini in large saucepan with water and extra oil, bring to boil, reduce heat to medium and cook for approximately 1 hour until zucchini are cooked—remove from heat and cool.

5.
Serve with Egg & Lemon Sauce (Avgolemono) (Page 38) made with zucchini stock.

MOUSSAKA
SERVES 6 - 8

MOUSSAKA

	Metric/Imp.	U.S.
Eggplant	*1.5kg/3lb*	*3 lb*
Salt		

MEAT SAUCE

Olive oil	*125ml/4fl oz*	*½ cup*
Butter	*50g/2oz*	*3 tbsp*
Mince steak	*1kg/2lb*	*2 lb*
Large onions, grated	*2*	*2*
Garlic cloves, crushed	*3*	*3*
Peeled, canned tomatoes plus liquid, chopped	*500g/1lb*	*2 cups*
Tomato paste	*60g/2oz*	*3 tbsp*
Cinnamon	*1 tsp*	*1 tsp*
Water	*185ml/6fl oz*	*¾ cup*
Salt and pepper		

CREAM SAUCE

Butter	*75g/3oz*	*⅓ cup*
Flour	*50g/2oz*	*6 tbsp*
Milk	*1ltr/2pts*	*4½ cups*
Eggs	*3*	*3*
Parmesan or kefalotiri cheese, grated	*60g/2oz*	*½ cup*
Salt and pepper		

EGGPLANT

1.

Wash eggplant and peel three strips off skin lengthways. Cut into 6mm/¼" thick slices and sprinkle with salt.

2.

Place slices in colander and stand for 30-45 minutes.

3.

Gently shake excess moisture from eggplant slices and place on greased baking trays in single layers. Bake approximately 30-40 minutes, turning once.

MEAT SAUCE

1.

Melt oil and butter in large frypan, add meat, onions and garlic and brown.

2.

Add remaining ingredients and simmer on low heat for 20-30 minutes.

CREAM SAUCE

1.

Melt butter in saucepan, remove from heat and add flour, stirring to a smooth paste. Return to medium heat and slowly add milk stirring constantly until sauce begins to bubble and thicken.

2.

Cook for 1-2 minutes, remove from heat and allow to cool slightly.

3.

Add eggs one at a time to sauce and stir quickly. Return to heat and add cheese, salt and pepper and mix well.

4.

Cook further 1-2 minutes until mixture bubbles.

TO ASSEMBLE MOUSSAKA

1.

Spread thin layer of cream sauce over bottom of large baking dish (33cm x 23cm x 5cm/13" x 9" x 2").

2.

Place a layer of eggplant slices over sauce and top with meat sauce. Place remainder of eggplant slices over meat.

3.

Spread cream sauce over eggplant and sprinkle with extra cheese and cinnamon.

4.

Bake in moderately hot oven for 1 hour until browned on top.

VARIATION I

Eggplant slices can be fried instead of baked but a large amount of oil is needed as eggplants tend to absorb a lot of oil during frying.

VARIATION II

Thin slices of potato can be substituted for eggplant to make potato moussaka, follow the rest of method above.

NOTE

Moussaka has more flavour if reheated and served the day after cooking. Serve with Greek Salad (Page 24) and crusty bread.

EGGPLANT LITTLE SHOES

SERVES 4

PAPOUTSAKIA

	Metric/Imp.	U.S.
Medium eggplants	1½kg/3lb	3 lb
Olive oil	250ml/8fl oz	1 cup
Mince beef or lamb	500g/1lb	1 lb
Large onion, grated	1	1
Garlic cloves, crushed	2	2
Large tomatoes, grated	2	2
Tomato paste	30g/1oz	1½ tbsp
Parsley, chopped	25g/1oz	¼ cup
Cinnamon	½ tsp	½ tsp
Salt and pepper		
Water	80ml/3fl oz	⅓ cup
Extra grated cheese		
Extra cinnamon		

CREAM SAUCE

	Metric/Imp.	U.S.
Butter	40g/1½oz	2½ tbsp
Flour	25g/1oz	3 tbsp
Milk	375ml/12fl oz	1½ cups
Parmesan cheese, grated	60g/2oz	½ cup
Eggs	2	2
Salt and pepper		

1.

Wash eggplants, remove stems and halve lengthways. Scoop out flesh, chop and reserve.

2.

Sprinkle inside eggplant shells with a little salt and stand 30 minutes.

3.

Heat oil in frypan, pat dry eggplants and gently fry on both sides until almost soft. Remove and set aside.

4.

Add mince, onion and garlic to oil, saute until meat is browned.

Add tomatoes, tomato paste, eggplant pulp, parsley, cinnamon, salt, pepper and water, simmer until sauce is thick.

5.

Place eggplant shells into large baking dish and stuff each one with meat filling.

6.

Spread cream sauce over each, sprinkle with extra grated cheese, cinnamon and put 250ml/ 8 fl oz/1 cup water into bottom of baking dish. Bake in moderately hot oven uncovered for 30-40 minutes.

TO MAKE CREAM SAUCE

1.

Melt butter, add flour, mix to a smooth paste and slowly add milk mixing constantly until sauce bubbles and thickens.

2.

Remove from heat, cool slightly and add cheese, mix well.

Add eggs one at a time stirring quickly and return to heat for 1-2 minutes until sauce bubbles and thickens. Add salt and pepper.

CABBAGE ROLLS IN EGG & LEMON SAUCE

SERVES 4 - 6

LAHANO DOLMATHES AVGOLEMONO

	Metric/Imp.	U.S.
Medium cabbage	½	½
Water		
Oil	*30ml/1fl oz*	*2 tbsp*
Butter	*50g/2oz*	*3 tbsp*
Salt and pepper		

STUFFING

Mince steak	*500g/1lb*	*1 lb*
Onions, grated	*2*	*2*
Tomatoes, grated— *reserve skin*	*3*	*3*
Parsley, chopped	*25g/1oz*	*¼ cup*
Rice	*125g/4oz*	*½ cup*
Butter	*50g/2oz*	*3 tbsp*
Olive oil	*60ml/2fl oz*	*¼ cup*

SAUCE

Butter	*50g/2oz*	*3 tbsp*
Flour	*35g/1½oz*	*4 tbsp*
Cabbage stock	*500ml/1pt*	*2½ cups*
Milk	*250g/8fl oz*	*1 cup*
Egg yolks, beaten	*2*	*2*
Lemon, juiced	*1*	*1*
Salt and pepper		

1.
Blanch cabbage in boiling, salted water for 5 minutes, drain and separate leaves.

2.
Mix all stuffing ingredients together.

3.
Cut cabbage leaves in two if large and place small amount of stuffing on each piece of cabbage. Roll up tightly.

4.
Place tomato skins in bottom of saucepan and layer cabbage rolls on top.

5.
Cover with water, oil, butter, salt and pepper and place small saucer on top of rolls to prevent them opening during cooking.

6.
Cover and cook for 40-50 minutes.
When cooked drain and reserve stock for sauce.

SAUCE
1.
Using butter, flour, stock and milk, prepare sauce as for White Cream Sauce (Page 40) then add eggs mixed with lemon juice, salt and pepper. Cook further 1-2 minutes.

2.
Arrange cabbage rolls on serving platter and pour sauce over.

STUFFED TOMATOES

SERVES 4 - 6

TOMATES YEMISTES

	Metric/Imp.	U.S.
Medium tomatoes	2kg/4lb	4 lb
Olive oil	60ml/2fl oz	¼ cup
Butter	50g/2oz	3 tbsp
Mince steak	500g/1lb	1 lb
Garlic cloves, crushed	3	3
Onions, grated	2	2
Tomato paste	30g/1oz	1½ tbsp
Parsley, chopped	25g/1oz	¼ cup
Rice, washed, drained	125g/4oz	½ cup
Salt and pepper		
Water	185ml/6fl oz	¾ cup
Breadcrumbs		
Parmesan cheese, grated		
Water, extra	500ml/1pt	2½ cups
Olive oil, extra	60ml/2fl oz	¼ cup

4.
Add 250g/8oz/1 cup chopped tomato pulp, tomato paste, parsley, rice, salt and pepper and mix well.

5.
Add water and cook on medium heat for 15-20 minutes.

6.
Fill each tomato with meat mixture, sprinkle with breadcrumbs and a little grated cheese and replace top of tomatoes.

7.
Place tomatoes in large baking dish side by side. Mix any remaining tomato pulp with extra oil and water, pour this over tomatoes and bake in moderately hot oven 1½ hours. Baste occasionally with juices. If necessary, add extra water.

1.
Slice off top of each tomato, scoop out and reserve pulp.

2.
Sprinkle inside tomatoes with a little salt, turn upside down and stand 10 minutes.

3.
Heat oil and butter in large frypan, brown mince, garlic and onion.

VARIATION
Capsicum and eggplants can be prepared the same way — discard pulp and use either chopped, peeled tomatoes or grated, fresh tomatoes. A combination of stuffed capsicum, tomatoes and eggplants is delicious.

MACARONI & MEAT PIE

SERVES 6 - 8

PASTITSIO

MEAT SAUCE

	Metric/Imp.	U.S.
Olive oil	60ml/2fl oz	¼ cup
Butter	50g/2oz	3 tbsp
Mince steak	1kg/2lb	2 lb
Medium onions, grated	2	2
Large ripe tomatoes, grated	3	3
Cinnamon	1½ tsp	1½ tsp
Water	125ml/4fl oz	½ cup
Salt and pepper		

CREAM SAUCE

Butter	75g/3oz	⅓ cup
Flour	100g/3oz	½ cup
Milk	1ltr/2pts	4½ cups
Eggs	2	2
Parmesan or kefalotiri cheese, grated	100g/3oz	¾ cup
Salt		
Macaroni - penne	375g/13oz	13 oz
Oil	3 tsp	3 tsp
Parmesan cheese, grated		
Cinnamon		

MEAT SAUCE

1.

Heat oil and butter in large frypan.
Brown mince, add onion, saute further 5 minutes.

2.

Add tomatoes, cinnamon, water, salt and pepper. Stir well.

3.

Cover and cook for 15-20 minutes until sauce thickens.

CREAM SAUCE

1.

Melt butter in large saucepan, remove from heat, add flour and mix to smooth paste. Return to medium heat.

Slowly add milk, stirring constantly with wooden spoon until sauce bubbles and thickens. Cook for 1-2 minutes.

Remove from stove and cool slightly.

2.

Crack eggs one at a time into sauce and whisk quickly.

Add cheese and salt, mix well, return to stove. Stir constantly till sauce begins to bubble and thicken. Remove from heat.

PASTITSIO

1.

Boil macaroni in salted water with 3 tsp oil until just tender but firm, drain.

2.

Spread bottom of large dish with layer of cream sauce. Spread half macaroni on top and stir slightly so macaroni are coated in cream. Top with meat sauce.

3.

Cover with remainder of macaroni and pour rest of sauce on top. Sprinkle with extra grated cheese and cinnamon. Bake in moderate-hot oven for 45 minutes, until well browned on top.

Pies

Pites

Καλή όρεχη

MEAT PIE

SERVES 4 - 6

KREATOPITA

	Metric/Imp.	U.S.
Olive oil	80ml/3fl oz	⅓ cup
Mince steak	1kg/2lb	2 lb
Large onions, halved and sliced	2	2
Water	80ml/3fl oz	⅓ cup
Eggs, beaten	4	4
Parmesan or kefalotiri cheese, grated	120g/4oz	1 cup
Black olives, pitted and halved	10-12	10-12
Salt and pepper		
Cumin	1 tsp	1 tsp
Sheets filo pastry	12	12
Melted butter		
Sesame seeds	25g/1oz	3 tbsp

1.
Heat oil in frypan, brown mince.

2.
Add onions, saute 2-3 minutes, add water, cook further 2 minutes.

3.
Remove from heat, add eggs, cheese, olives, salt, pepper and cumin, mix.

4.
Place six sheets filo pastry in baking dish (30cm x 19cm/12" x 8"), brushing each sheet with melted butter.

5.
Pour meat mixture over pastry, top with remaining sheets of filo, again brushing each sheet with melted butter.

6.
Score top 3 layers of filo in diamond shapes, brush with melted butter, sprinkle with water and sesame seeds.

7.
Bake in moderate-hot oven 45 minutes until golden brown.

8.
Serve with Greek Salad (Page 24).

CHEESE PIE

TIROPITA

	Metric/Imp.	U.S.
Feta cheese, grated	375g/12oz	12 oz
Cottage cheese	250g/8oz	1 cup
Oregano	2 tsp	2 tsp
Butter	40g/1½oz	2 tbsp
Flour	25g/1oz	3 tbsp
Milk	375ml/12floz	1½ cups
Parmesan cheese, grated	60g/2oz	½ cup
Eggs	2	2
Pepper		
Butter, extra	125g/4oz	½ cup
Sheets filo pastry	15	15
Sesame seeds	1 tsp	1 tsp

1.
Combine feta and cottage cheese with oregano.

2.
Melt butter in saucepan, add flour and stir into thick paste. Slowly add milk, stirring constantly until sauce thickens and bubbles, add parmesan cheese, cool slightly.

3.
Add eggs one at a time, beat quickly and return to heat for 1 minute until sauce is very thick, add pepper.

4.
Combine cheese mixture and cream sauce, mixing well.

5.
Melt extra butter, grease bottom of baking pan and line with 8 sheets of filo pastry, brushing each sheet with butter.

6.
Pour in cheese mixture and cover with remaining filo, brushing each sheet with butter.

7.
Trim and tuck sides of pastry, prick top with fork.
  Brush with melted butter and sprinkle with a little water and sesame seeds.

8.
Bake in moderately hot oven 30-40 minutes until golden brown.

133

SPINACH PIE WITH RICE

S E R V E S 4

SPANAKOPITA ME RIZI

	Metric/Imp.	U.S.
Package frozen puff pastry	1	1
Rice	185g/6oz	¾ cup
Bunch spinach, chopped	1	1
Salt	1 tsp	1 tsp
Olive oil	125ml/4fl oz	½ cup
Pepper		
Melted butter		
Sesame seeds		

1.

Thaw pastry at room temperature.

2.

Soak rice in boiling water for 5 minutes, drain.

3.

Wash spinach, drain in colander, sprinkle with salt leave 5 minutes.

4.

Squeeze spinach repeatedly with hands to drain all moisture.

5.

Place spinach in mixing bowl with onions, rice, oil and pepper and mix well.

6.

Roll out 2 sheets 6mm/¼" thick pastry to fit baking dish 30cm x 19cm/12" x 8". Brush with melted butter.

7.

Place one sheet on bottom of dish and spread spinach mixture on top. Cover with remaining pastry.

8.

Prick pastry with fork 5-6 times and brush with melted butter, sprinkle with water and sesame seeds.

9.

Bake in moderate oven 45-60 minutes.

VARIATION

Use any extra pastry sheets to make individual small spanakopitas. Roll each sheet and cut into desired sized circles. Place filling in centre, fold over and seal edges. Brush with butter, sprinkle with water and sesame seeds.

CHEESE TURNOVERS

MAKES APPROX 45

TIROPITES APO ZIMI

PASTRY

	Metric/Imp.	U.S.
Butter	250g/8oz	1 cup
Hot water	250g/8fl oz	1 cup
Vegetable oil	250g/8fl oz	1 cup
Self-raising flour	825g/1lb13oz	6½ cups

FILLING

Feta cheese, finely crumbled	375g/13oz	13 oz
Cottage cheese	375g/13oz	13 oz
Eggs, beaten	2	2
Oregano	3 tsp	3 tsp

PASTRY

1.

Cut butter into 5-6 pieces and add to hot water in bowl, stir until butter dissolves.

2.

Add oil, mix well and add flour.

3.

Mix to form dough, knead for approximately 2 minutes. (This pastry is extremely quick and easy to make and a very workable consistency.)

FILLING

Mix all ingredients together.

PREPARATION

1.

Roll out pastry to 6mm/¼" thickness and cut into 11cm/4½" rounds.

2.

Place 1 tsp of filling in centre and fold over, press ends together.

3.

Brush each turnover with beaten egg, sprinkle sesame seeds on top.

4.

Place on greased trays and bake in hot oven for approximately 20 minutes until golden brown.

NOTE

This type of "Tiropites" is quick and easy to prepare and can be eaten warm or cold so are great for picnics, school lunches, parties etc. They can be made smaller or larger according to the occasion. Tiropites freeze well. Bake frozen for approximately 25-30 minutes.

SPINACH PIE
SERVES 4

SPANAKOPITA

	Metric/Imp.	U.S.
Large bunch spinach	1	1
Salt	2 tsp	2 tsp
Olive oil	125ml/4fl oz	½ cup
Large onion, grated	1	1
Shallots, chopped	8	8
Eggs	3	3
Feta cheese, grated	300g/12oz	12 oz
Parmesan cheese, grated	25g/1oz	¼ cup
Freshly ground black pepper		
Butter, melted	125g/4oz	½ cup
Filo pastry	250g/8oz	8 oz
Sesame seeds	25g/1oz	3 tbsp

1.
Wash spinach, cut off most stems, chop and place in colander. Sprinkle with salt, mix with hands and let stand for 20 minutes.

2.
Heat oil in large saucepan, add onion and shallots and gently fry.

3.
Squeeze spinach to drain excess moisture, add to saucepan and cook 10 minutes. Remove from heat and cool.

4.
Beat eggs, add cheeses, pepper and spinach and mix well.

5.
Brush bottom and sides of baking dish 33cm x 23cm x 5cm/13" x 9" x 2", with melted butter and line with half the filo pastry, brushing each sheet with melted butter.

6.
Add spinach filling on top and cover with remaining filo, brushing each sheet with butter. Trim and tuck edges.

Brush top with melted butter, sprinkle with a little water (this prevents top layers of filo from curling during cooking).

7.
Sprinkle with sesame seeds and bake in moderately hot oven 45 minutes or until golden brown and crisp.

Spinach Pie

QUICK CHEESE PIE

SERVES 4

TIROPITA TIS STIGMIS

	Metric/Imp.	U.S.
Feta cheese, grated	200g/7oz	7 oz
Cottage cheese	375g/12oz	1½ cups
Parmesan cheese, grated	25g/1oz	¼ cup
Eggs, beaten	3	3
Oregano	1½ tsp	1½ tsp
Freshly ground black pepper		
Melted butter		
Sheets ready rolled puff pastry	2	2
Sesame seeds		

1.

Mix together feta, cottage and parmesan cheese.

2.

Add eggs, oregano and pepper and mix well.

3.

Brush bottom of pie plate with melted butter, line with one sheet of pastry and pour mixture on top.

4.

Cover with other pastry sheet, brush with butter, sprinkle with water and sesame seeds.

5.

Bake in moderately hot oven for 20-30 minutes until pastry is golden brown.

NOTE

Can be prepared in advance and frozen before cooking.

Quick Cheese Pie
Village Tomato Salad (see p. 20)

CHICKEN PIE

SERVES 4 - 6

KOTOPITA

	Metric/Imp.	U.S.
Chicken, boiled	1.5kg/3lb	3 lb
Butter	40g/1½oz	2 tbsp
Large onion, chopped	1	1
Shallots, chopped	4	4
Garlic cloves, crushed	2	2
Bacon rashers, chopped	3	3
Parsley, chopped	25g/1oz	3 tbsp
Nutmeg	½ tsp	½ tsp
Salt and pepper		
Butter, extra	50g/2oz	3 tbsp
Sheets filo pastry	10	10
Sesame seeds		

CREAM SAUCE

	Metric/Imp.	U.S.
Butter	40g/1½oz	2 tbsp
Flour	25g/1oz	3 tbsp
Milk	375ml/12oz	1½ cups
Parmesan cheese, grated	60g/2oz	½ cup
Eggs	2	2
Salt and pepper		

1.

Skin and debone cooked chicken and chop into small pieces.

2.

Melt butter, add onion, shallots, garlic and saute. Add bacon and parsley, saute further 3-4 minutes. Remove from heat.

3.

Add chicken pieces, nutmeg, salt and pepper, mix well set aside.

4.

Prepare cream sauce, fold into chicken, mix well.

5.

Grease pie plate with extra butter and line with 5 sheets of filo pastry, brushing each sheet with melted butter. Pour chicken mixture on top and cover with remaining 5 sheets of pastry, brushing each with butter.

6.

Trim and tuck edges of pastry, brush top with butter, sprinkle with a little water and sesame seeds. Bake in moderately hot oven for approximately 30 minutes until golden brown.

CREAM SAUCE

1.

Melt butter, add flour, mix to smooth paste and slowly add milk, mixing constantly until sauce bubbles and thickens. Cool slightly, add cheese, stir, add eggs one at a time stirring quickly.

2.

Return to heat for 1-2 minutes until sauce thickens add salt and pepper.

VARIATION

2 sheets of prepared ready rolled puff pastry can be substituted for filo pastry. Follow same method and alter cooking time accordingly.

SAVOURY TART

TOURTA ALMIRI

PASTRY

	Metric/Imp.	U.S.
Butter	*150g/5oz*	*⅔ cup*
Egg yolk	*1*	*1*
Flour	*225g/7oz*	*1½ cups*
Salt		
Baking powder	*1 tsp*	*1 tsp*

CREAM MIXTURE

	Metric/Imp.	U.S.
Egg yolks, beaten	*6*	*6*
Flour	*25g/1oz*	*3 tbsp*
Milk	*500ml/1pt*	*2½ cups*
Gruyere cheese, grated	*50g/2oz*	*½ cup*
Parmesan cheese, grated	*25g/1oz*	*¼ cup*
Freshly ground black pepper		
Paprika	*½ tsp*	*½ tsp*

PASTRY

1.
Melt butter, cool and mix with egg.

2.
Sift flour, salt and baking powder and add to butter mixture.

3.
Knead to form a soft dough and roll out to cover bottom of pie plate or ovenproof baking dish. If pastry too flaky press into dish with your hands.

CREAM MIXTURE

1.
Mix all ingredients together and pour into pie plate lined with pastry.

2.
Sprinkle with extra pepper and paprika and bake in moderately hot oven 1-1¼ hours until set and golden brown. Stand for one hour before cutting.

Cakes, Sweets & Biscuits

Glykismata

Καλή όρεχη

RUM BABA

SERVES 8-12

BABAS

	Metric/Imp.	U.S.
Eggs	4	4
Sugar	250g/8oz	1 cup
Vanilla essence	1 tsp	1 tsp
Self-raising flour	200g/7oz	1⅔ cups
Fresh cream		

SYRUP

	Metric/Imp.	U.S.
Sugar	500g/1lb	2 cups
Water	185ml/6fl oz	¾ cup
Rum	185ml/6fl oz	¾ cup
Piece lemon rind	1	1

SYRUP

Boil all ingredients together for 3 minutes, cool completely. Strain.

CAKE

1.

Beat eggs until frothy, add sugar, beat until light and fluffy.

2.

Add vanilla essence and sifted flour, beat for 3 minutes.

3.

Pour into ring form baking pan and cook in moderate oven for 30-40 minutes until cake is light brown in colour.

4.

Remove from oven and pour cold syrup on top. Stand in tin until ready to serve (at least 2 hours).

5.

Remove from tin and place on serving dish, decorate with whipped cream.

HONEY COATED
CRISP FRIED PASTRY

MAKES APPROX 3 ½ DOZ

XEROTIGANA

	Metric/Imp.	U.S.
Unsalted butter	125g/4oz	½ cup
Eggs	2	2
Plain flour	450g/15oz	3 cups
Orange juice	60ml/2fl oz	¼ cup
Water	60ml/2fl oz	¼ cup
Icing/powdered sugar		
Cinnamon		
Coarsely ground walnuts	125g/4oz	4 oz

SYRUP

Honey	450g/15oz	1½ cups
Honey extra	60ml/2fl oz	¼ cup

1.

Beat butter and eggs until light and fluffy.

2.

Add flour, orange juice and water, knead to form a soft dough.

3.

Roll into paper-thin rectangles and shape as below.

4.

Fry in hot oil until golden and pastry rises to surface—approximately 1 minute (turning once).

5.

Dip quickly into warm syrup and arrange pastry in piles on a serving dish. Sprinkle each layer with icing/powdered sugar, cinnamon and walnuts.

SYRUP

Heat honey and water and keep warm.

TO SHAPE PASTRY

1.

Cut into strips 20cm/8" long by 2.5cm/1" wide.

2.

Press pastry together at intervals of 2.5cm/1" and wind around to form a rosette, press edges together. *or* As above but do not wind to form rosette. *or* Cut strips 12cm/4½" long and press pastry together in middle to form bow ties.

143

CARMELINA'S CHOCOLATE MARBLE CAKE

KEIK ME SOKOLATA

	Metric/Imp.	U.S.
Unsalted butter	*250g/8oz*	*1 cup*
Sugar	*425g/14oz*	*1¾ cups*
Eggs	*4*	*4*
Grated rind one orange		
Whisky	*20ml/1fl oz*	*1½ tbsp*
Self-raising flour, sifted	*450g/15oz*	*3 cups*
Warm milk	*185ml/6fl oz*	*¾ cup*
Orange juice	*60ml/2fl oz*	*¼ cup*
Cocoa	*25g/1oz*	*3 tbsp*

1.
Beat butter and sugar until light and fluffy.

2.
Add eggs one at a time, beating well after each addition.

3.
Add orange rind and whisky, mix well.

4.
Beat in flour with milk and orange juice.

5.
Place ⅔ of mixture into well greased and floured ring form tin.

6.
Mix cocoa into remaining ⅓ of mixture and pour into tin.

7.
Swirl chocolate mixture through with a pointed knife.

8.
Bake in moderate-hot oven 40-45 minutes. Cool before turning out.

GRAPE JUICE PUDDING

SERVES 4

MOUSTALEVRI

	Metric/Imp.	U.S.
Grape juice	750ml/1¼ pts	2½ cups
Sugar	3 tsp	3 tsp
Water	80ml/3fl oz	⅓ cup
Rice flour	25g/1oz	¼ cup
Cinnamon	½ tsp	½ tsp
Whipped cream		
Cinnamon, extra		

1.

Bring grape juice and sugar to boil.

2.

Mix water, rice flour and cinnamon until smooth.

3.

Slowly pour flour mixture into grape juice, stirring constantly until it thickens and bubbles.

4.

Pour into individual serving dishes and chill for a few hours before serving with whipped cream and extra cinnamon.

ALMOND SHORTBREAD BISCUITS

MAKES APPROX 2½ DOZ

KOURAMBIETHES

	Metric/Imp.	U.S.
Blanched almonds	125g/4oz	4 oz
Oil	1 tsp	1 tsp
Butter, unsalted	250g/8oz	1 cup
Icing/powdered sugar	25g/1oz	4 tbsp
Ouzo	30ml/1fl oz	2 tbsp
Vanilla essence	1 tsp	1 tsp
Egg yolk	1	1
Plain flour	375g/14oz	2⅔ cup
Baking powder	1 tsp	1 tsp

1.
Coat almonds in oil and roast in oven 5-10 minutes until light golden brown, crush.

2.
Melt butter in saucepan until colour just begins to change, place in mixing bowl and leave to cool.

3.
Beat butter well, add 25g/1oz/4 tbsp icing/powdered sugar, ouzo and vanilla and beat.

4.
Add egg and almonds, mix well, gradually add sifted flour and baking powder.

5.
Knead mixture lightly, mould dough into half moon shapes.

6.
Place on ungreased baking trays and bake in moderately hot oven for 15-20 minutes.

7.
Allow to cool in trays for 2-3 minutes. Remove and place on waxed paper which has been thickly dusted with icing/powdered sugar.

8.
Whilst still warm, sift icing sugar over biscuits making sure they are well coated all over. Cool completely before storing in airtight containers. Extra icing sugar may be added before serving.

GREEK COCONUT CAKE

KEIK ME KARITHA

	Metric/Imp.	U.S.
Unsalted butter	250g/8oz	1 cup
Sugar	500g/1lb	2 cups
Eggs	6	6
Shredded coconut	225g/7oz	2½ cups
Vanilla essence	1 tsp	1 tsp
Self-raising flour	325g/11oz	2½ cups
Milk	375ml/12fl oz	1½ cups

SYRUP

	Metric/Imp.	U.S.
Water	750ml/1¼pts	3 cups
Sugar	625g/1lb 4oz	2¾ cups
Lemon, juiced	1	1

1.
Cream butter and sugar until light and fluffy.

2.
Add eggs one at a time, beating well after each addition.

3.
Add coconut and vanilla essence, mix well.

4.
Add flour alternating with milk, mix well.

5.
Pour into large well greased square cake tin and cook in moderate oven for 1-1½ hours until cake is cooked when tested.

6.
Place syrup ingredients in large saucepan and bring to boil, boil for 5 minutes then leave to cool.

7.
Cut hot cake into serving pieces, leave in baking tin, pour cold syrup over hot cake.

8.
Stand for several hours before serving, until cake cools completely and has absorbed syrup.

NUT-FILLED BISCUITS
MAKES APPROX 2½ DOZ

MOSKOPOUNDIA

	Metric/Imp.	U.S.
Unsalted butter	125g/4oz	½ cup
Oil	125ml/4fl oz	½ cup
Milk	125ml/4fl oz	½ cup
Water	60ml/2fl oz	¼ cup
Plain flour		
Baking powder	1 tsp	1 tsp
Icing/powdered sugar		

FILLING

	Metric/Imp.	U.S.
Walnuts, ground	125g/4oz	4 oz
Almonds, ground	125g/4oz	4 oz
Nutmeg	1 tsp	1 tsp
Cinnamon	1 tsp	1 tsp
Sugar	250g/8oz	1 cup
Water	185ml/6fl oz	¾ cup

1.
Combine filling ingredients in a saucepan and cook 10-15 minutes. Set aside.

2.
Melt butter, add to oil, milk, water and baking powder and mix.

3.
Add as much flour as necessary to make a workable dough that is not sticky.

4.
Roll out dough to 6mm/¼" thickness and cut into 5cm/2" circles.

5.
Place spoonfuls of filling in centre of each circle, fold and press together edges.

6.
Place on greased baking trays and bake in moderately hot oven for 10-15 minutes.

7.
Remove from tray and place on waxed paper or large platter and sprinkle liberally with icing/powdered sugar all over whilst still hot.

8.
Cool completely before storing in airtight container.

NOTE

These will keep for several weeks if stored properly.

LATTICED
APRICOT SLICE

PASTA FLORA

	Metric/Imp.	U.S.
Unsalted butter	250g/8oz	1 cup
Sugar	175g/6oz	¾ cup
Egg	1	1
Flour	450g/15oz	3 cups
Apricot conserve	375g/12oz	1¼ cups

1.
Cream butter and sugar until light and fluffy, add egg and mix 1-2 minutes.

2.
Add flour and knead by hand to a smooth dough.

3.
Line bottom of greased baking tray approximately 31cm x 26cm x 4cm /10" x 12" x 1½") with 2/3 of pastry.

4.
Press pastry down with hands and spread conserve on top.

5.
Roll remainder of pastry into long pencil-shaped rolls and place diagonally on top of conserve, forming lattice design and then around edges of baking tray.

6.
Bake in moderate-hot oven approximately ½ hour until lattice golden brown.

149

CUSTARD SLICE

GALATOMBOURIKO

	Metric/Imp.	U.S.
Milk	750ml/1½pts	3 cups
Eggs	4	4
Sugar	175g/6oz	¾ cup
Rice flour	50g/2oz	½ cup
Vanilla essence	1½ tsp	1½ tsp
Unsalted butter	25g/1oz	1½ tbsp
Sheets filo pastry	16	16
Unsalted butter, extra	50g/2oz	3 tbsp

SYRUP

	Metric/Imp.	U.S.
Water	500ml/1pt	2½ cups
Sugar	250g/8oz	1 cup
Lemon juice	1½ tsp	1½ tsp
Cinnamon stick	1	1
Strip lemon rind	1	1

SYRUP

Bring all ingredients to boil, boil 10 minutes and cool.

SLICE

1.
Boil milk, cool. Beat eggs and sugar until frothy, add rice flour and vanilla.

2.
Return milk to medium heat, slowly pour egg mixture into milk and stir with wooden spoon until mixture thickens, add butter, stir.

3.
Brush dish (20cm x 30cm x 5cm / 8" x 12" x 2") with melted butter and place 8 sheets filo pastry in bottom, brushing each sheet with melted butter.

4.
Spoon custard into dish, top with remaining sheets of filo brushing each with butter, trim and tuck edges.

5.
Brush top filo sheet with butter, score top layers of filo into diamond or square shapes and sprinkle with water. Bake in moderate oven 45 minutes until golden brown.

6.
Remove cinnamon and lemon rind from syrup and pour over hot pie and let cool before serving.

EASTER BREAD

MAKES ONE LARGE TSOUREKI

TSOUREKI

	Metric/Imp.	U.S.
Dry yeast	3 tsp	3 tsp
Lukewarm milk	185ml/6fl oz	¾ cup
Plain flour	650g/1½lb	5 cups
Mixed spice	1¼ tsp	1¼ tsp
Eggs	3	3
Sugar	175g/6oz	¾ cup
Rind 1 lemon		
Unsalted butter, melted	200g/7oz	7 oz
Vanilla essence	1 tsp	1 tsp
Coloured hard boiled egg (optional)	1	1
Egg, beaten, for glazing	1	1
Sesame seeds		

1.

Dissolve yeast in half quantity of milk.

2.

Sift flour and mixed spice into a bowl, make a well in the centre.

3.

Beat eggs, add sugar and mix for 1 minute.

4.

Add lemon rind, butter, vanilla essence, remainder of milk and yeast mixture, mix well.

5.

Pour into centre of flour and gently blend together with hands.

6.

Turn onto floured surface and knead for 8-10 minutes. Shape into a round ball.

7.

Brush top of dough with melted butter and place in a bowl that has also been brushed with melted butter .

8.

Cover with a cloth and leave to rise until doubled in size (if weather is cool, cover with a blanket for extra warmth).

9.

Punch down dough, turn out onto floured surface and knead for 2-3 minutes.

10.

Divide dough into 3 equal pieces, roll each one into 15" strips and form a thick plait. Alternatively you can roll each piece longer and plait, bringing ends together to form a plaited ring.

11.

Insert a coloured hard boiled egg into one of the folds or centre of ring and place on a greased tray and leave to rise again for 1-2 hours.

12.

Brush with beaten egg, sprinkle with sesame seeds and cook in pre-heated moderate oven for 30-40 minutes until a deep golden brown.

CHOCOLATE BISCUIT LOG

KORMOS SOKOLATA

	Metric/Imp.	U.S.
Unsalted butter	*250g/8oz*	*1 cup*
Egg yolk	*1*	*1*
Icing/powdered sugar	*2 tsp*	*2 tsp*
Warm milk	*30ml/1fl oz*	*1½ tbsp*
Cognac	*30ml/1fl oz*	*1½ tbsp*
Cocoa	*25g/1oz*	*¼ cup*
Plain sweet biscuits, broken into small pieces	*125g/4oz*	*4 oz*
Icing sugar, extra	*50g/2oz*	*½ cup*
2 sheets waxed paper (approx 40cm/16" long)		

1.
Beat butter and egg yolk until light and fluffy.

2.
Add icing sugar, milk, cognac and cocoa, mix well.

3.
Fold in biscuits and mix well until biscuits are coated in chocolate cream.

4.
Place waxed paper on work bench and sprinkle with extra icing sugar to cover area approx 35cm/14" long.

5.
Shape biscuit mixture into a log approx 32cm x 5cm/13" x 2".

6.
Place log on icing sugar and roll until well covered.

7.
Lightly wrap in waxed paper, twist ends to seal and refrigerate overnight before serving. Cut into slices 2.5cm/1" wide.

Easter Bread (see p. 151)
New Year Bread (see p. 158)

GREEK DONUTS

KOULOURAKIA TIGANITA

	Metric/Imp.	U.S.
Eggs	2	2
Oil	*50ml/1½ fl oz*	*3 tbsp*
Sugar	*25g/1oz*	*2 tbsp*
Flour		
Icing/powdered sugar		
Cinnamon		
Oil, extra		

1.
Beat eggs, oil and sugar, add enough flour to form soft dough.

2.
Take small balls of dough and roll into pencil-thick strips and shape into rings.

3.
Heat oil, drop donuts into oil and fry until golden brown on both sides. (Donuts will float in oil when cooked).

4.
Remove from oil, place in dish and sprinkle with icing/powdered sugar and cinnamon.

NOTE
Donuts will keep in an airtight container for several days.

Carmelina's Chocolate Marble Cake (see p. 144)

Baklava (see p. 159)

Almond Shortbread Biscuits (see p. 146)

Latticed Apricot Slice (see p. 149)

Honey Cookies (see p. 154)

Chocolate Biscuit Log (see p. 152)

Sesame Biscuits (see p. 156)

Grape Juice Pudding (see p. 145)

HONEY COOKIES

MAKES APPROX 4 DOZ

MELOMAKARONA

	Metric/Imp.	U.S.
Oil	375ml/12fl oz	1½ cups
Sugar	250g/8oz	1 cup
Orange, juiced	1	1
Brandy	80ml/3fl oz	⅓ cup
Cinnamon	1½ tsp	1½ tsp
Baking powder	2 tsp	2 tsp
Plain flour	550g/1lb 3oz	4½ cups
Chopped walnuts	125g/4oz	1 cup
Cinnamon, extra		

SYRUP

	Metric/Imp.	U.S.
Sugar	250g/8oz	1 cup
Honey	300g/10oz	1 cup
Water	185ml/6fl oz	¾ cup
Cinnamon sticks	2	2

1.

Beat oil and sugar until thick and frothy.

2.

Add orange juice, brandy, cinnamon, baking powder and beat well.

3.

Slowly add enough flour until dough becomes workable and does not stick.

4.

Take walnut-sized pieces of dough and roll into thick oblong shapes.

5.

Place on greased baking tray (not too close together) and press each cookie down with a fork.

6.

Bake in moderate oven 20-30 minutes until golden brown.

Remove from oven and cool on wire rack.

7.

Dip and soak cookies a few at a time in hot syrup 10-15 seconds. Remove and arrange on platter.

Sprinkle each layer with coarsely ground walnuts and sprinkle liberally with cinnamon.

SYRUP

Place all ingredients in large saucepan, bring to boil and boil for 5 minutes. Remove from heat.

RICE PUDDING
S E R V E S 4

RIZOGALO

	Metric/Imp.	U.S.
Rice	185g/6oz	¾ cup
Water	250ml/8fl oz	1 cup
Sugar	175g/6oz	¾ cup
Vanilla essence	1 tsp	1 tsp
Milk	1ltr/2pts	4½ cups
Cornflour	2 tsp	2 tsp
Cinnamon		

1.
Place rice and water in saucepan, bring to boil, simmer covered 5-7 minutes.

2.
Add sugar, mix well and stir in vanilla, milk and cornflour (dissolve cornflour in a little milk first).

3.
Bring to boil, reduce heat and simmer 30 minutes.

4.
Place in large bowl or individual serving dishes and sprinkle liberally with cinnamon, chill and serve.

SESAME BISCUITS

MAKES APPROX 8 DOZ

	Metric/Imp.	U.S.
Butter	*250g/8oz*	*1 cup*
Sugar	*500g/1lb*	*2 cups*
Eggs	*4*	*4*
Vanilla essence	*2 tsp*	*2 tsp*
Cinnamon	*1½ tsp*	*1½ tsp*
Ground cloves	*½ tsp*	*½ tsp*
Self-raising flour	*750g/1lb10oz*	*6 cups*
Sesame seeds	*250g/8oz*	*1½ cups*
Eggs, beaten, extra	*2*	*2*

1.

Cream butter and sugar until light and fluffy.

2.

Beat in eggs one at a time, add vanilla and spices.

3.

Add flour a little at a time and mix to form soft dough (knead for 1 minute with hands — if needed add more flour).

4.

Break pieces of dough the size of a small walnut and form into twists and rings (roll each piece, fold over, twist then form into ring or roll out, fold over and twist).

5.

Roll each biscuit into the sesame seeds and coat thickly.

6.

Place on well greased baking trays and glaze each with beaten egg. Bake in moderately hot oven for approximately 30 minutes until deep golden brown. Cool before storing.

NOTE

These biscuits keep for weeks in an airtight container and are excellent with tea and coffee. Children love them.

Depending on the weather, dough may flake during shaping. If this happens, knead the biscuit a little. It is best to roll biscuits in sesame seeds as soon as they are shaped.

HONEY PUFFS

LOUKOUMATHES

	Metric/Imp.	U.S.
Dry yeast	*2 tsp*	*2 tsp*
Warm water	*500ml/1pt*	*2½ cups*
Sugar	*1 tsp*	*1 tsp*
Plain flour	*450g/1lb*	*3½ cups*
Honey	*450g/15oz*	*1½ cups*
Water	*80ml/3fl oz*	*1⅓ cups*
Oil		
Cinnamon		
Icing/powdered sugar		

1.

Dissolve yeast in 125ml/4fl oz/½ cup warm water in a mixing bowl.

2.

Add 1 tsp sugar, sifted flour, remaining warm water and beat with electric mixer until smooth.

3.

Cover with a clean cloth and set aside in a warm place to rise for 2-3 hours until mixture bubbles and doubles in size.

4.

Mix honey and water in saucepan, heat until well combined and keep hot.

5.

Heat oil until very hot, drop in heaped teaspoonfuls of mixture a few at a time and fry until puffed and golden brown—remove with slotted spoon.

6.

Dip each puff quickly into hot honey mixture, coating well, place on a serving platter and sprinkle with icing/powdered sugar and cinnamon. Serve hot/warm.

NOTE
The dough when ready is very sticky and elastic. Be careful as hot honey will drip when eaten.

NEW YEAR BREAD

VASILOPITA

	Metric/Imp.	U.S.
Dry yeast	3 tsp	3 tsp
Lukewarm milk	250ml/8fl oz	1 cup
Flour	750g/1lb 10oz	6 cups
Cinnamon	1¼ tsp	1¼ tsp
Nutmeg	½ tsp	½ tsp
Eggs	3	3
Sugar	250g/8oz	1 cup
Grated orange rind	1	1
Butter, melted	150g/5oz	⅔ cup
Coin wrapped in foil		
Egg, beaten, extra	1	1
Sesame seeds		

1.

Dissolve yeast in half the quantity of milk.

2.

Sift flour and spices into a bowl and make a well in centre.

3.

Beat eggs, add sugar and mix 1 minute.

4.

Add orange rind, melted butter, rest of milk and yeast mixture, stir well.

Pour mixture into centre of flour and gently blend together with hands.

5.

Turn onto floured surface and knead 8-10 minutes — shape into round ball and brush top with melted butter.

6.

Place dough in a bowl also brushed with melted butter and cover with cloth, leave to rise until doubled in size (if weather is cool, cover with blanket for extra warmth).

7.

Punch dough down, turn out onto floured surface and knead for 2-3 minutes.

Reserve a little of the dough.

8.

Shape dough into one large round cake and insert washed coin wrapped well in foil, into dough (Do not choose a very small coin in case of accidental swallowing).

9.

Roll out reserved dough to form numbers representing the New Year and press firmly in centre of cake.

Place into well-greased 34cm/13" round cake tin and leave to rise for 1-2 hours.

10.

Brush with beaten egg, sprinkle with sesame seeds and bake in pre-heated moderately hot oven for approximately 45 minutes until a deep shiny brown in colour.

NOTE

Dough can be divided to make two small New Year breads. New Year bread is traditionally cut at midnight at the start of the New Year. The bread is cut into one slice for the household, and one slice for each person present. Whoever gets the coin is supposed to have a very lucky year.

BAKLAVA

BAKLAVA

	Metric/Imp.	U.S.
Walnuts, finely chopped	*300g/10oz*	*10 oz*
Almonds, finely chopped	*200g/7oz*	*7oz*
Ground cinnamon	*2½ tsp*	*2½ tsp*
Ground cloves	*¼ tsp*	*¼ tsp*
Sugar	*75g/3oz*	*⅓ cup*
Butter, melted	*200g/7oz*	*¾ cup*
Sheets filo pastry	*30*	*30*

SYRUP

Sugar	*750g/1½lb*	*3 cups*
Water	*500ml/1pt*	*2½ cups*
Cinnamon sticks	*2*	*2*
Honey	*150g/5oz*	*½ cup*
Lemon juice	*40ml/1½fl oz*	*3 tbsp*
Whole cloves	*5*	*5*
Piece lemon rind	*1*	*1*

1.

Mix together nuts, cinnamon, cloves and sugar—set aside.

2.

Brush baking dish 33cm x 23cm x 5cm/13" x 9" x 2" with melted butter.

3.

Line bottom of dish with 10 sheets of filo, brushing each sheet with melted butter.

4.

Spread one third of nut mixture evenly on top and cover with another 5 sheets of filo, brushing each sheet with melted butter.

5.

Place half the remaining mixture on top of filo add 5 more sheets of filo. Repeat this step once more, using remainder of filo brushing each sheet with butter.

6.

Trim and tuck edges of pastry, brush top with butter and with a sharp knife score through top layers of filo in diamond shapes and sprinkle lightly with water (this prevents top layer of pastry from curling during cooking).

7.

Bake in moderate-hot oven approx 45 minutes until golden brown. Remove from oven and slowly pour cool strained syrup over hot baklava.

8.

Let stand several hours or overnight before serving.

TO MAKE SYRUP

1.

Combine all ingredients, heat and stir until sugar dissolves.

2.

Bring to boil and boil briskly for 8 minutes.

3.

Strain and cool before pouring over hot baklava.

Index